IF Found please return to....

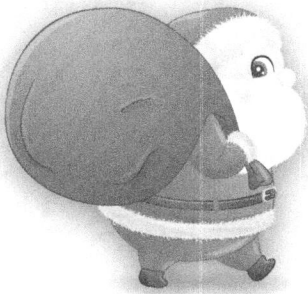

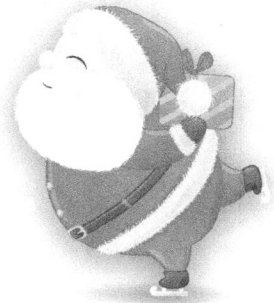

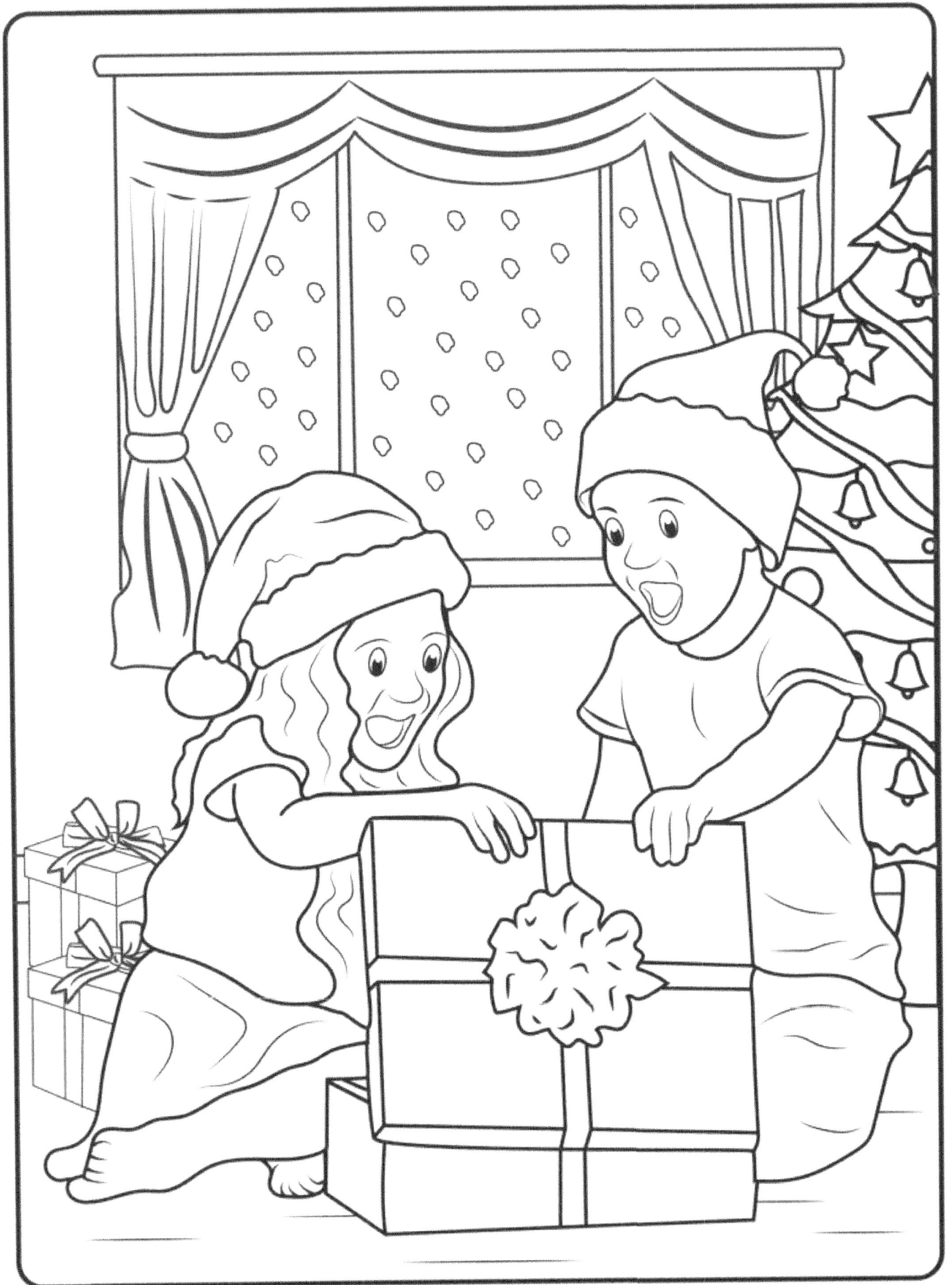

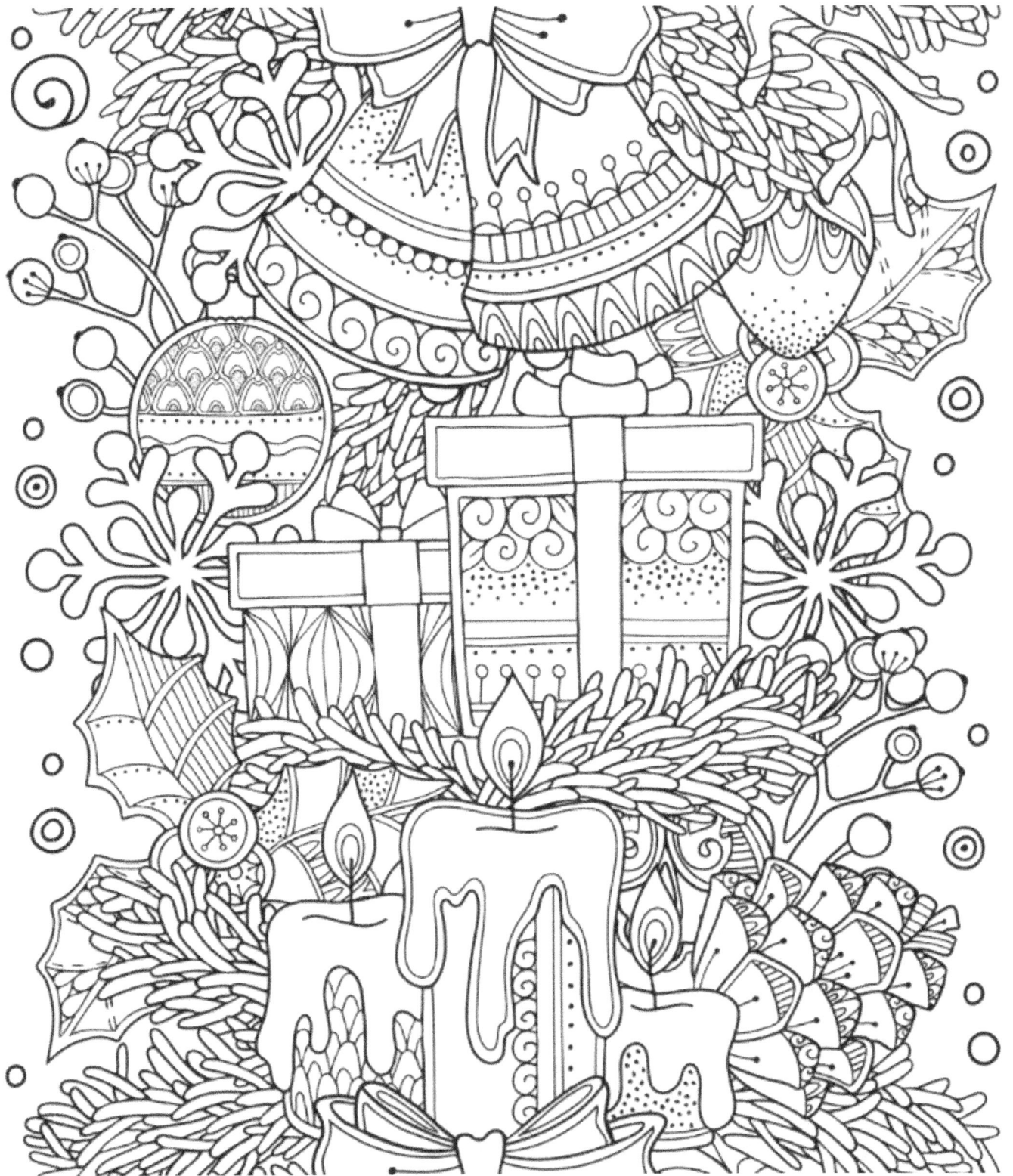

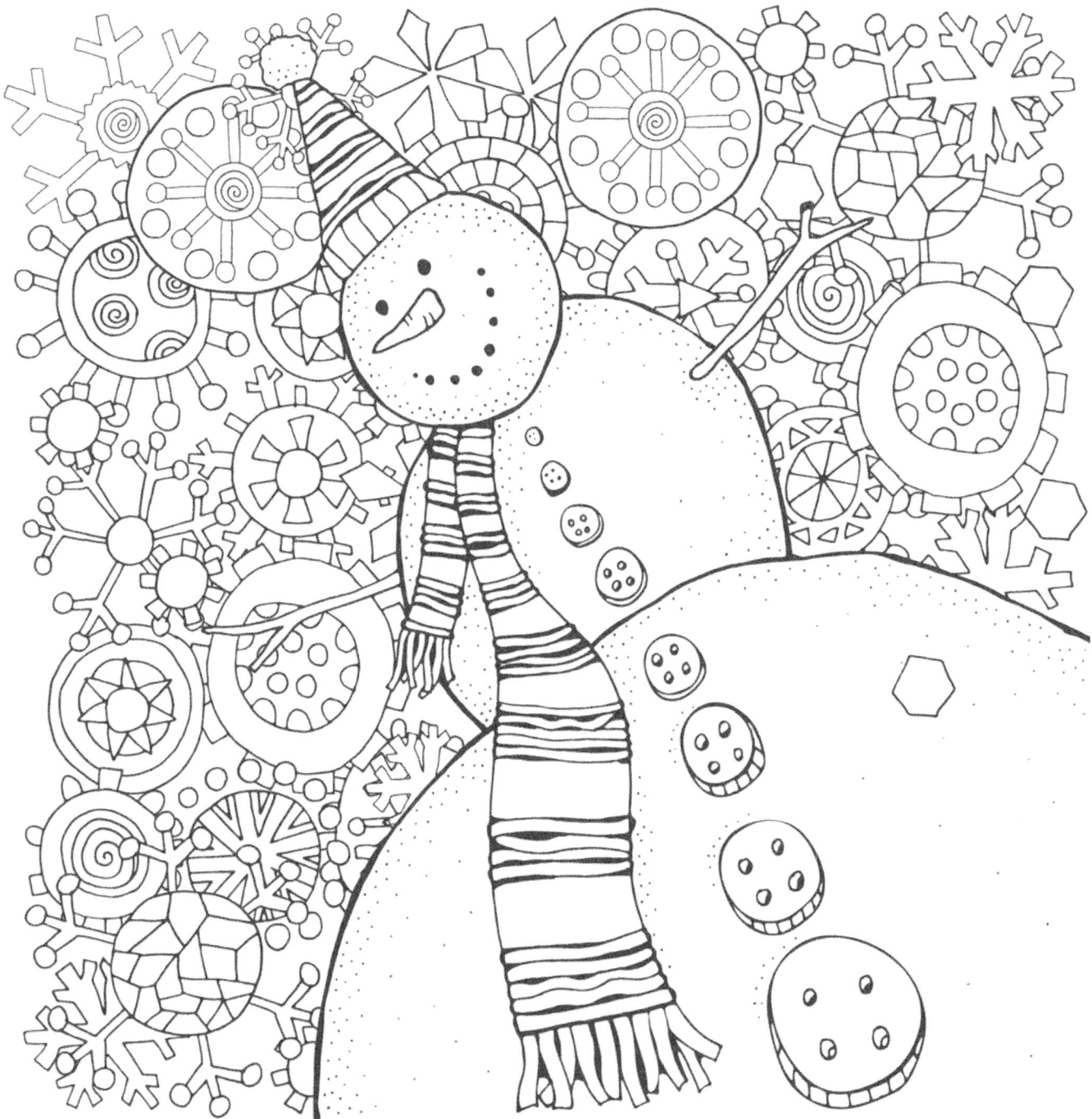

Merry Christmas

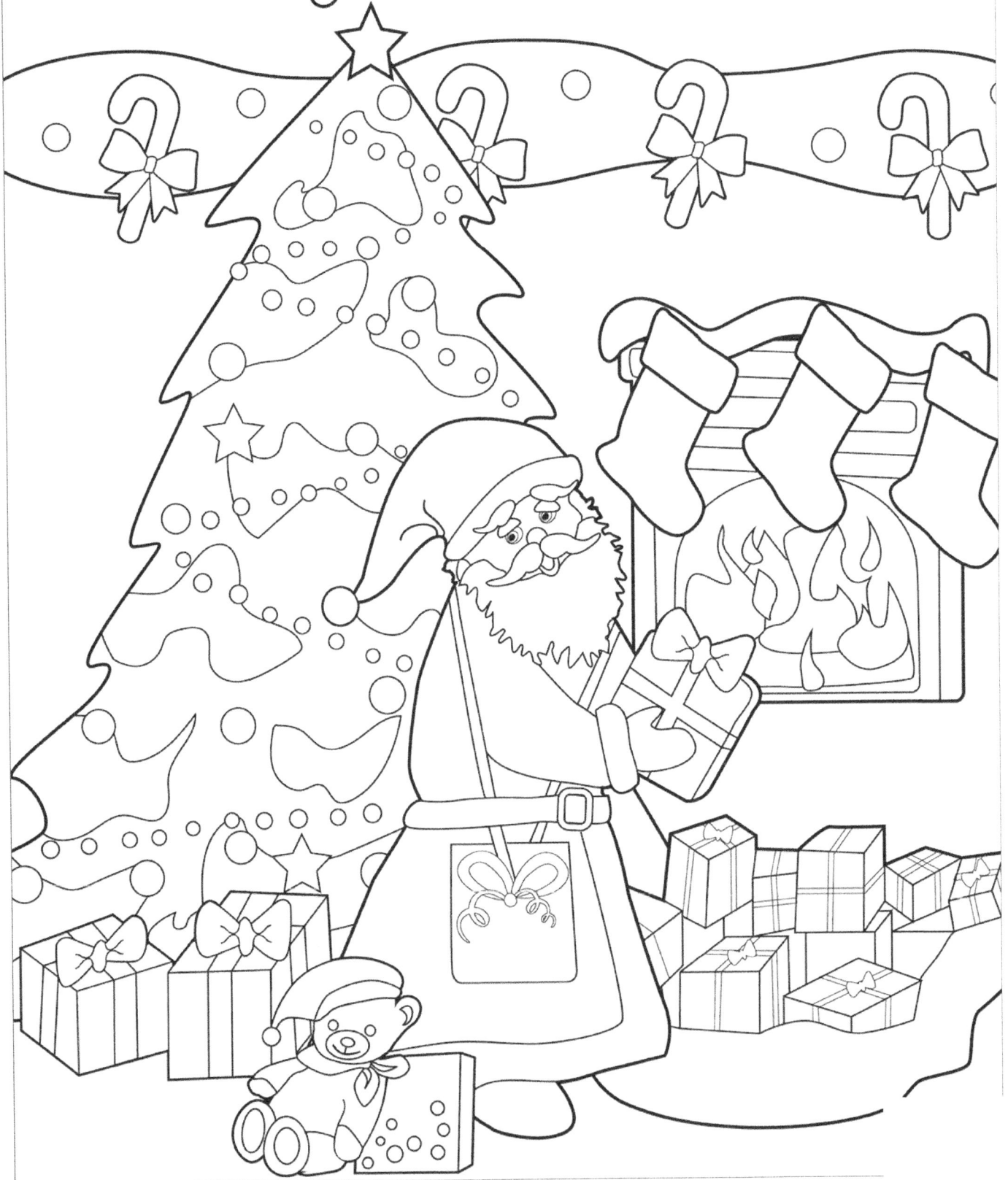

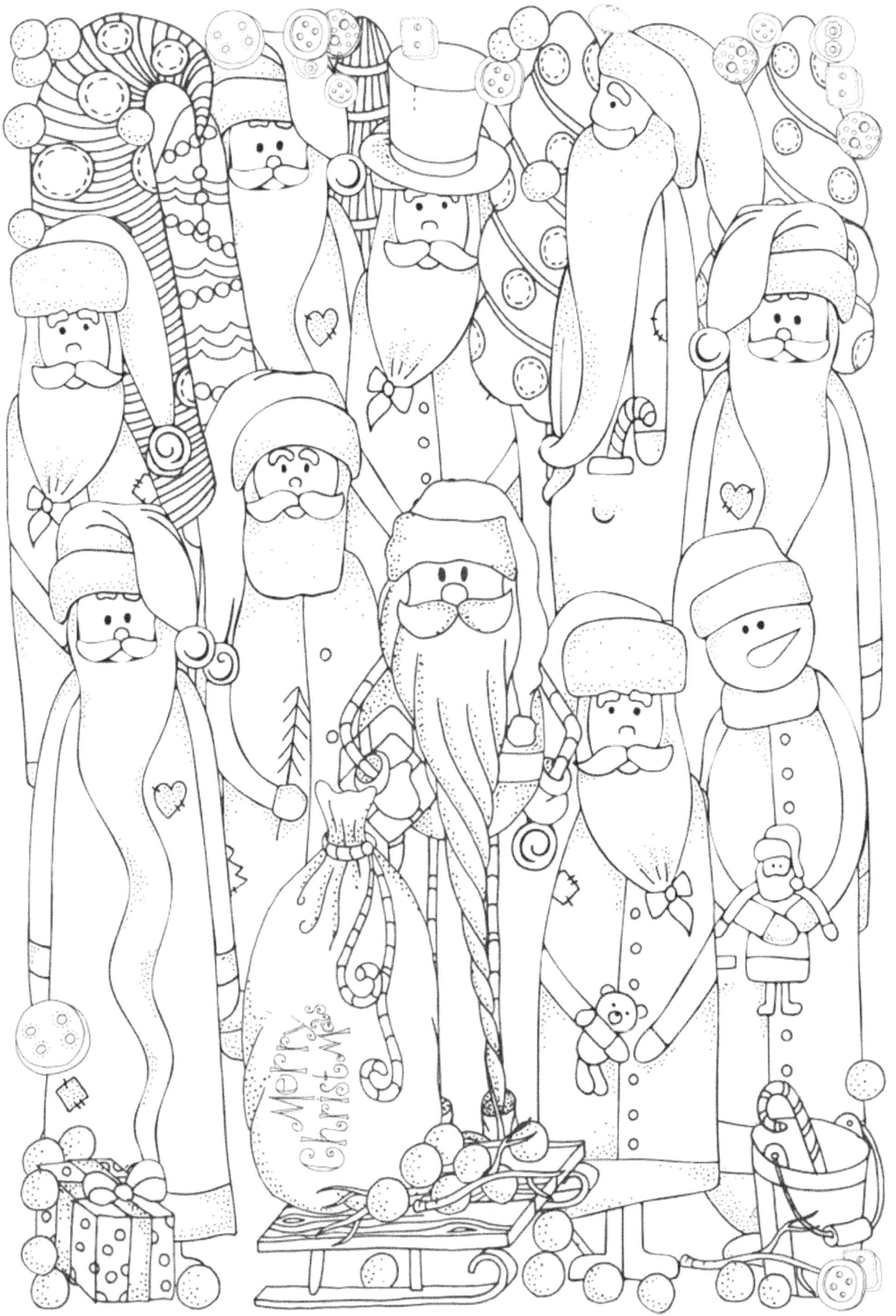

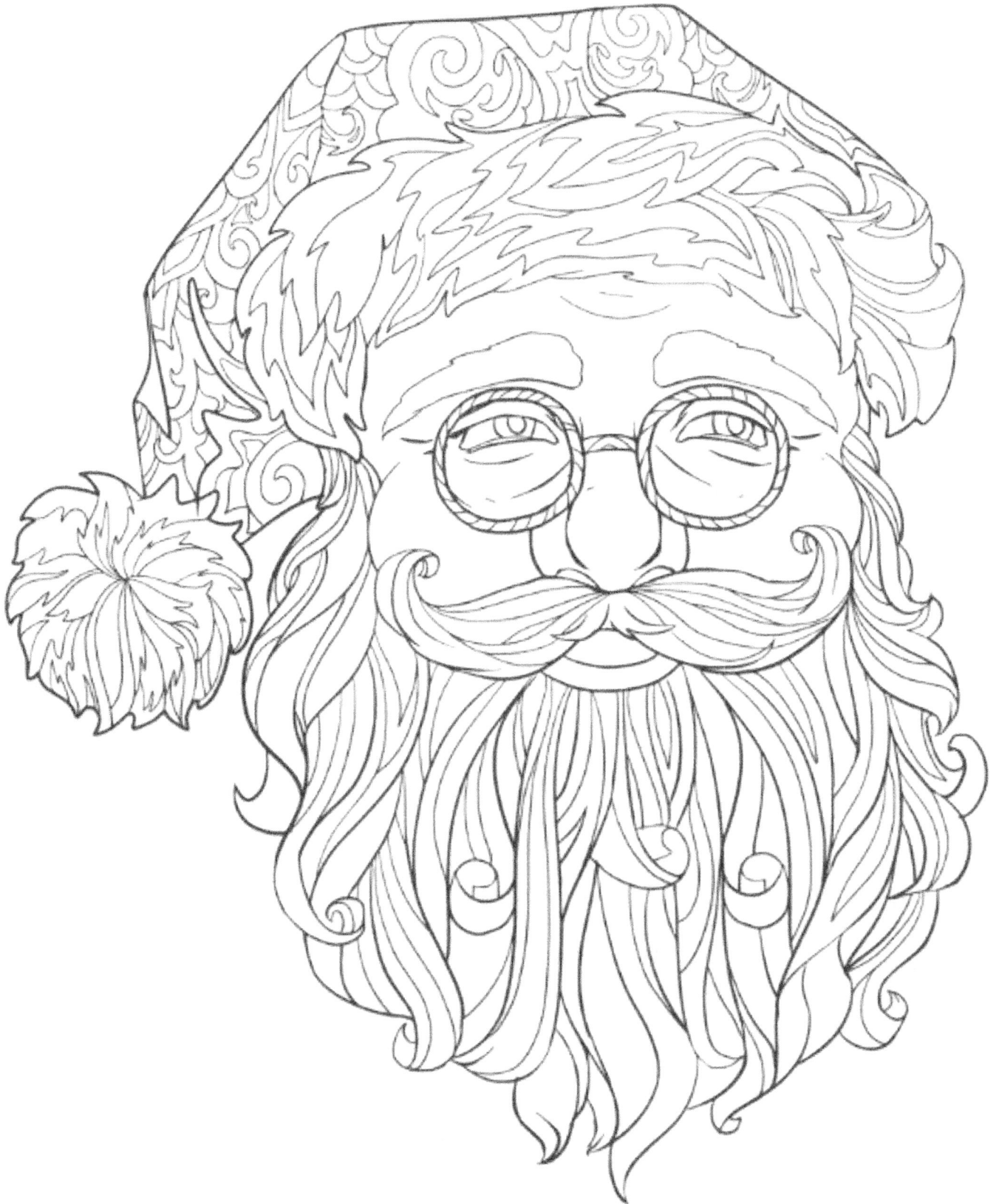

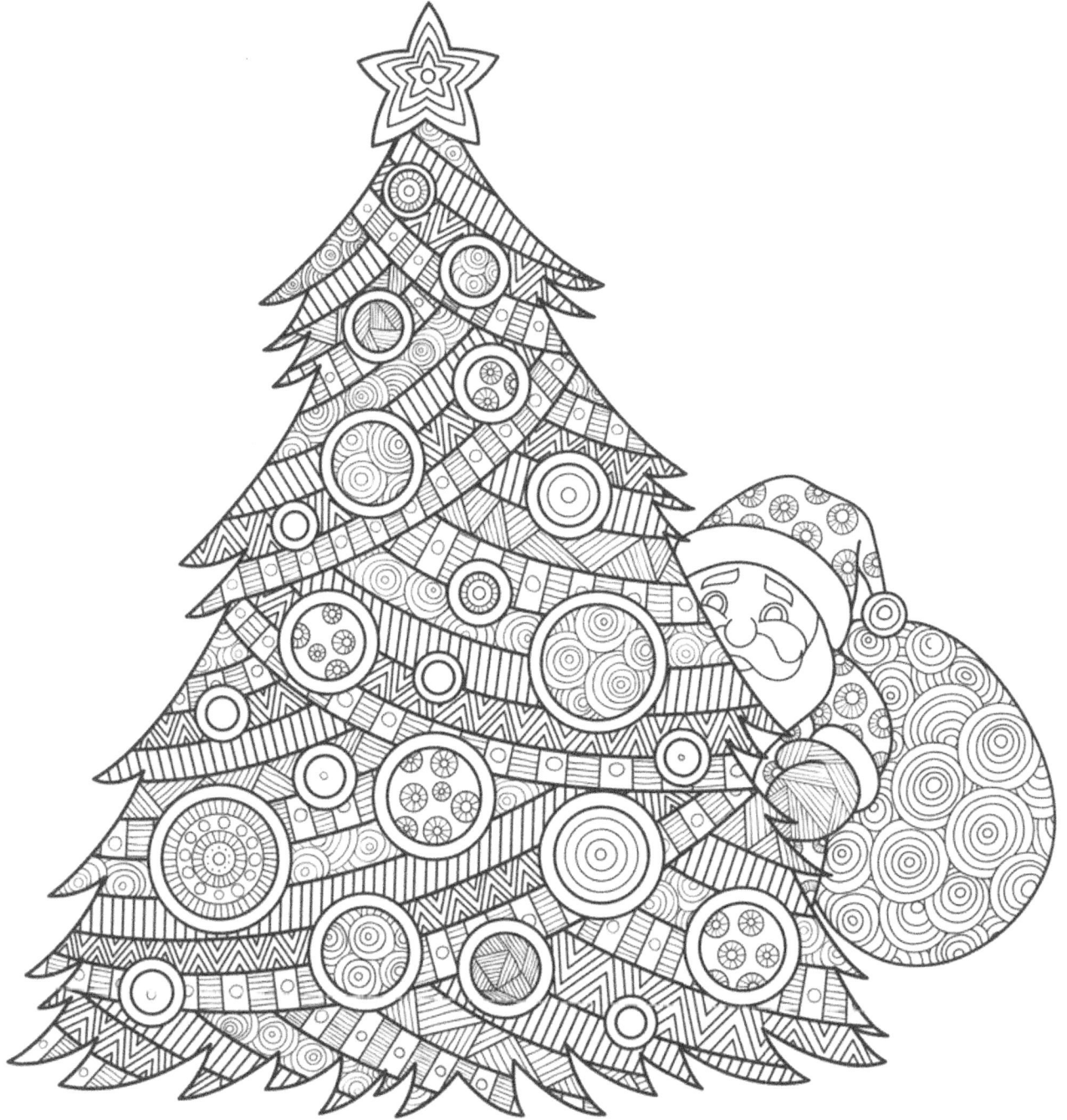

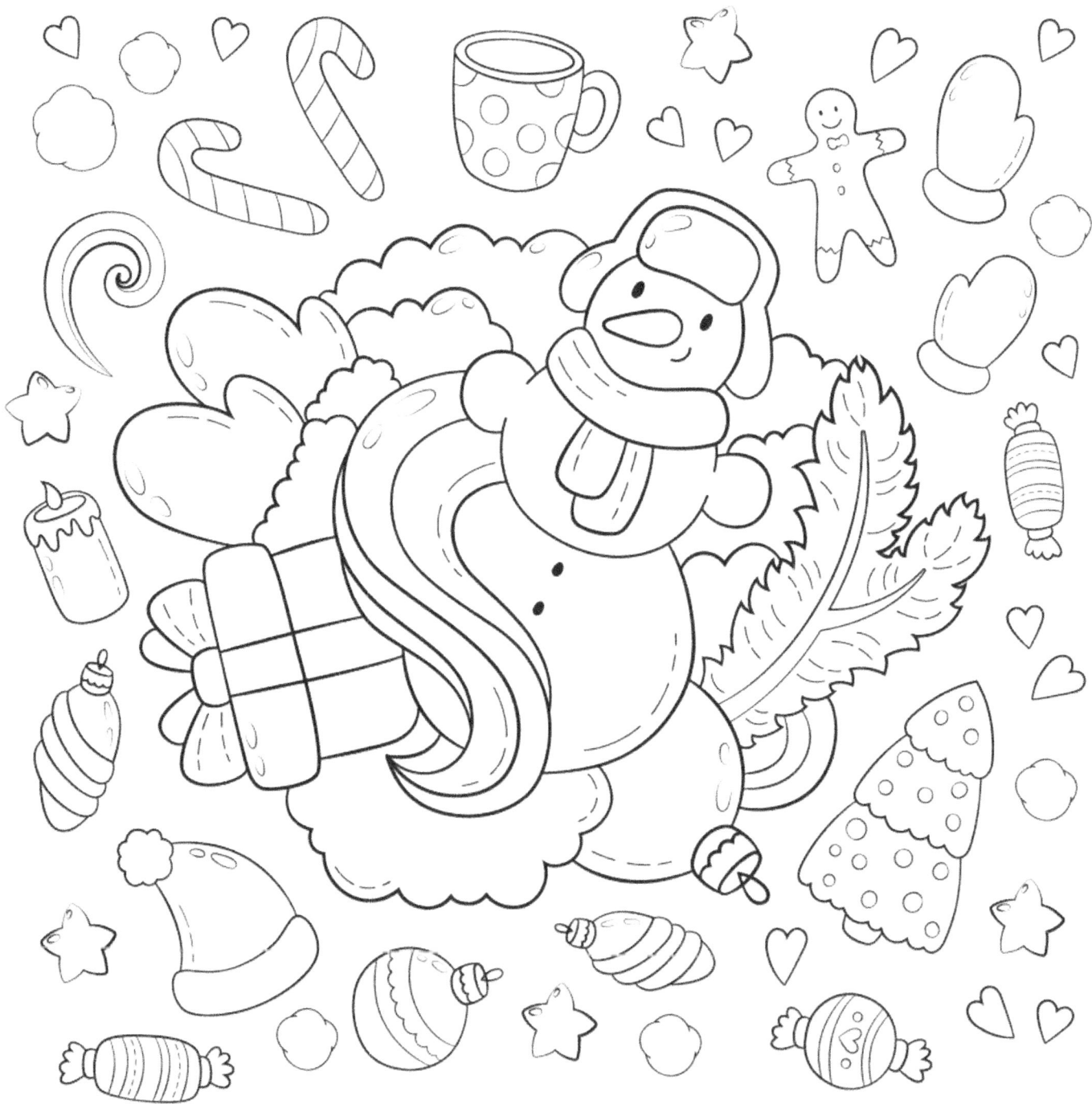

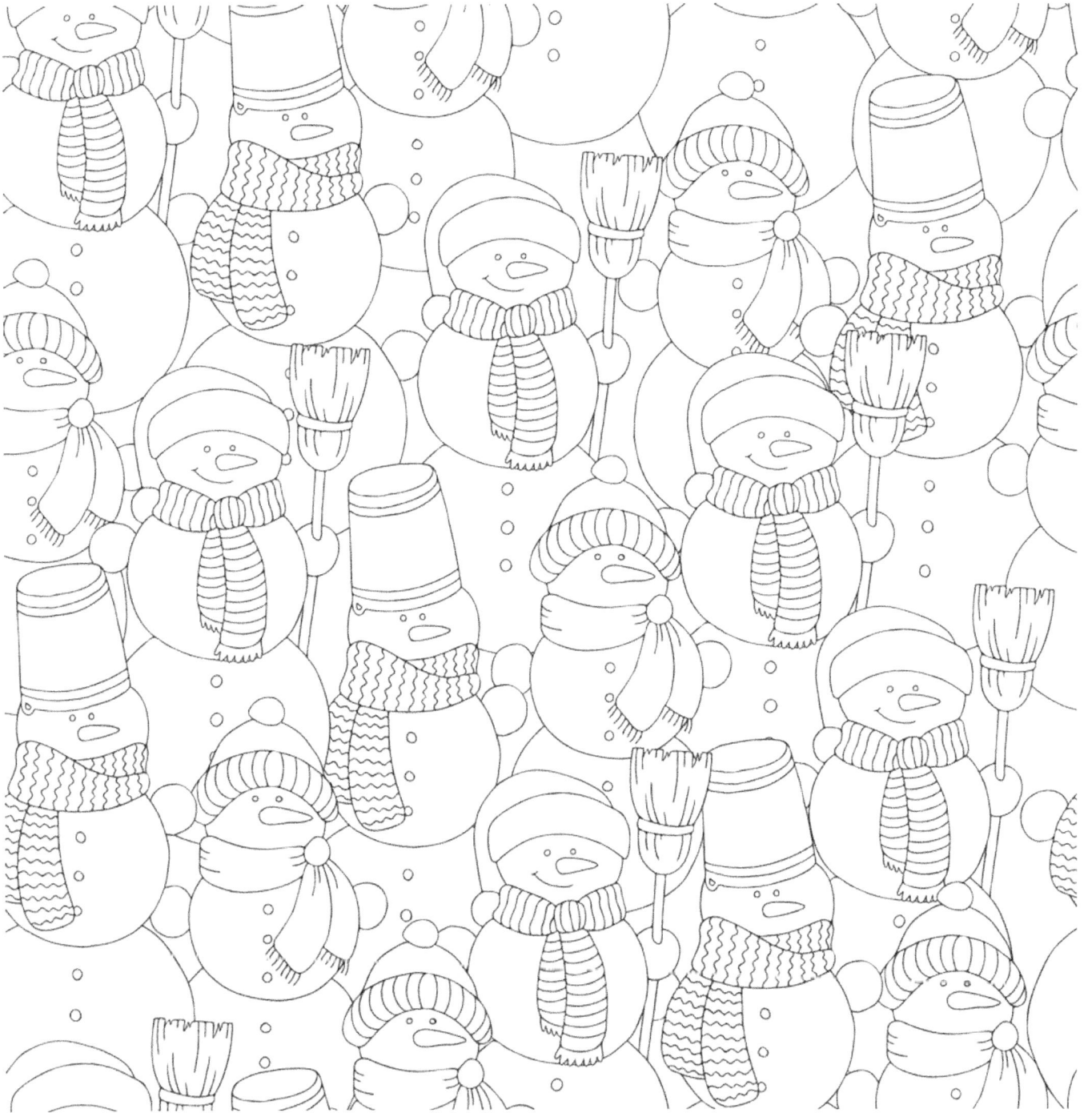

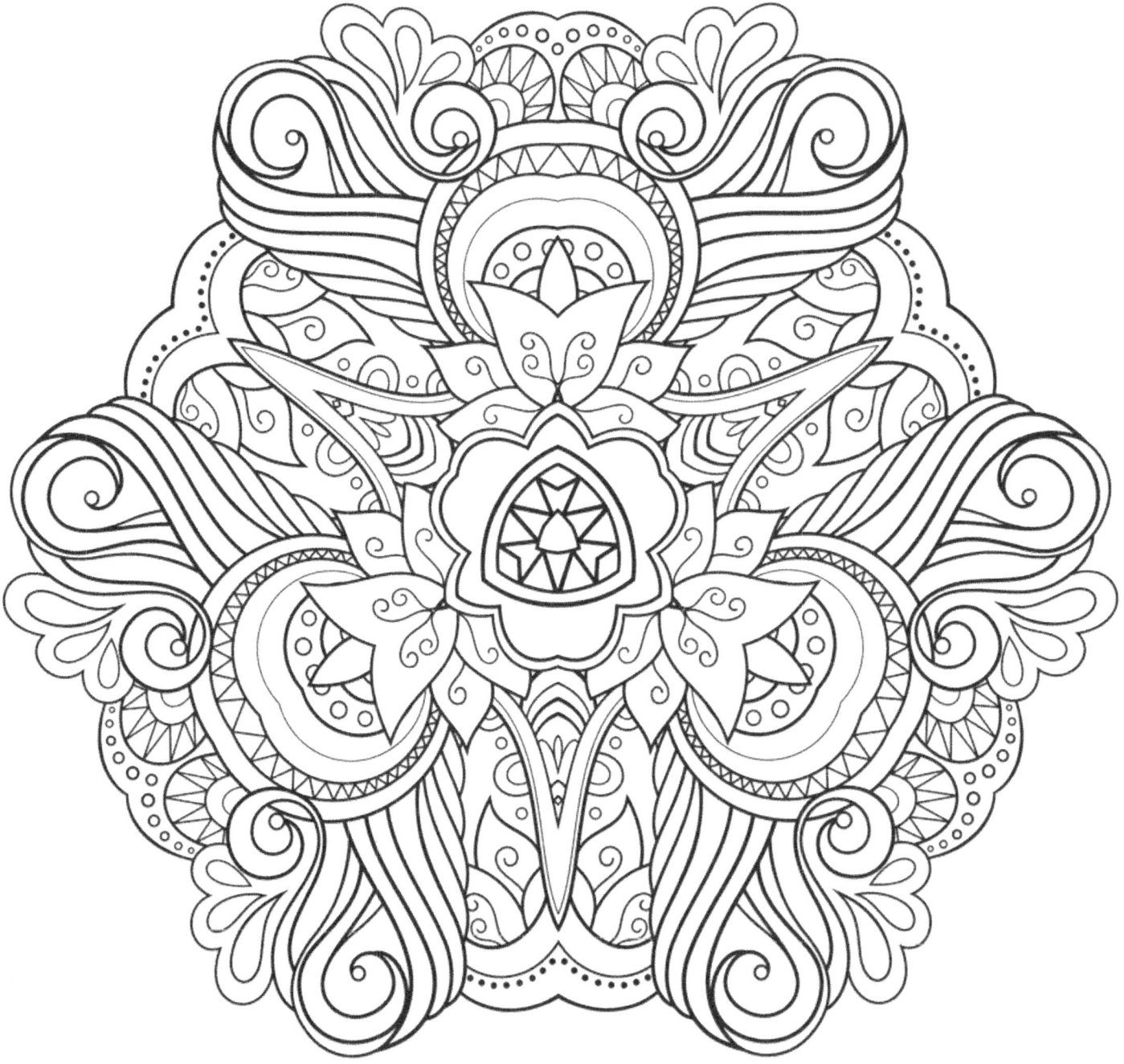

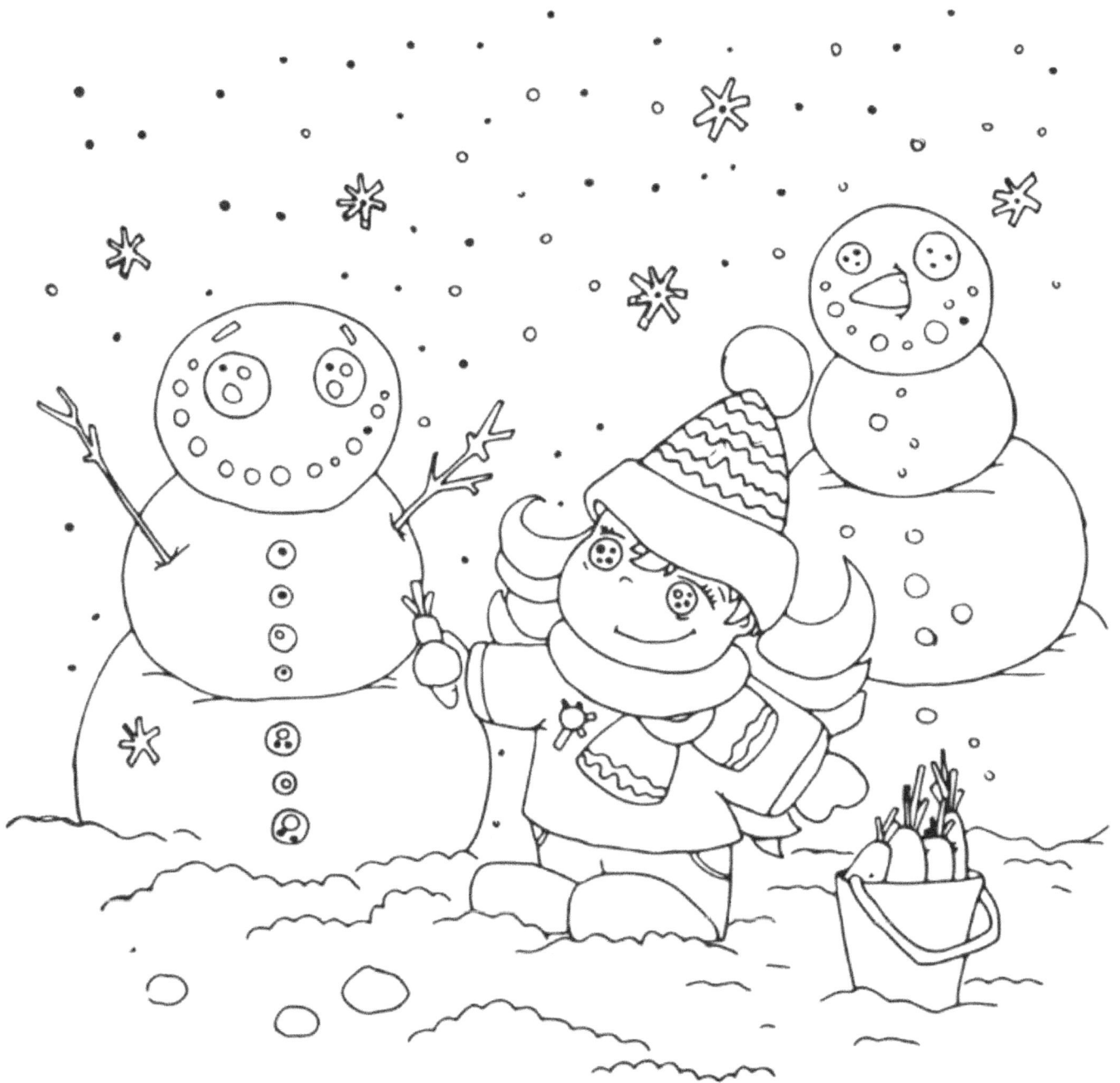

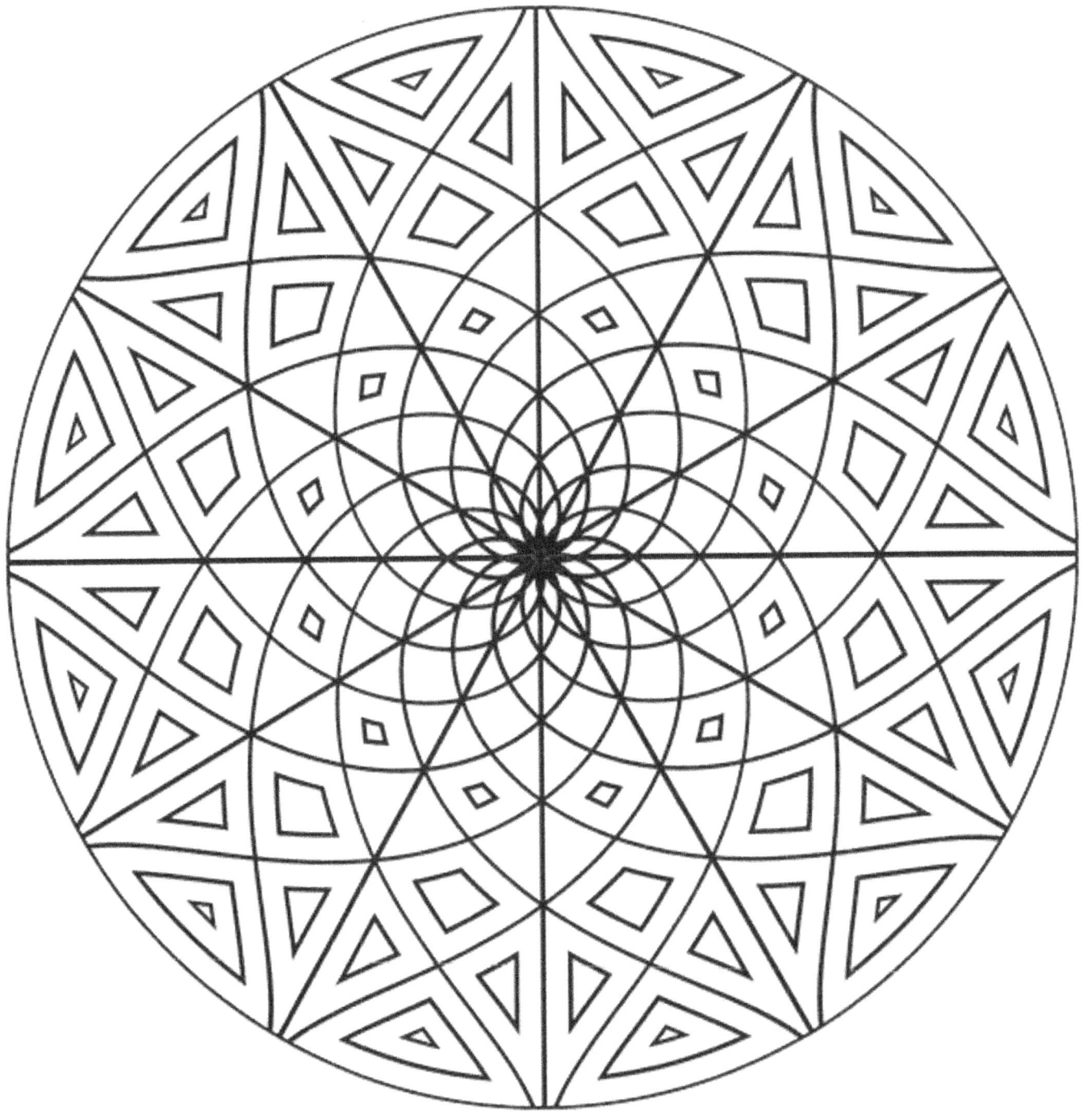

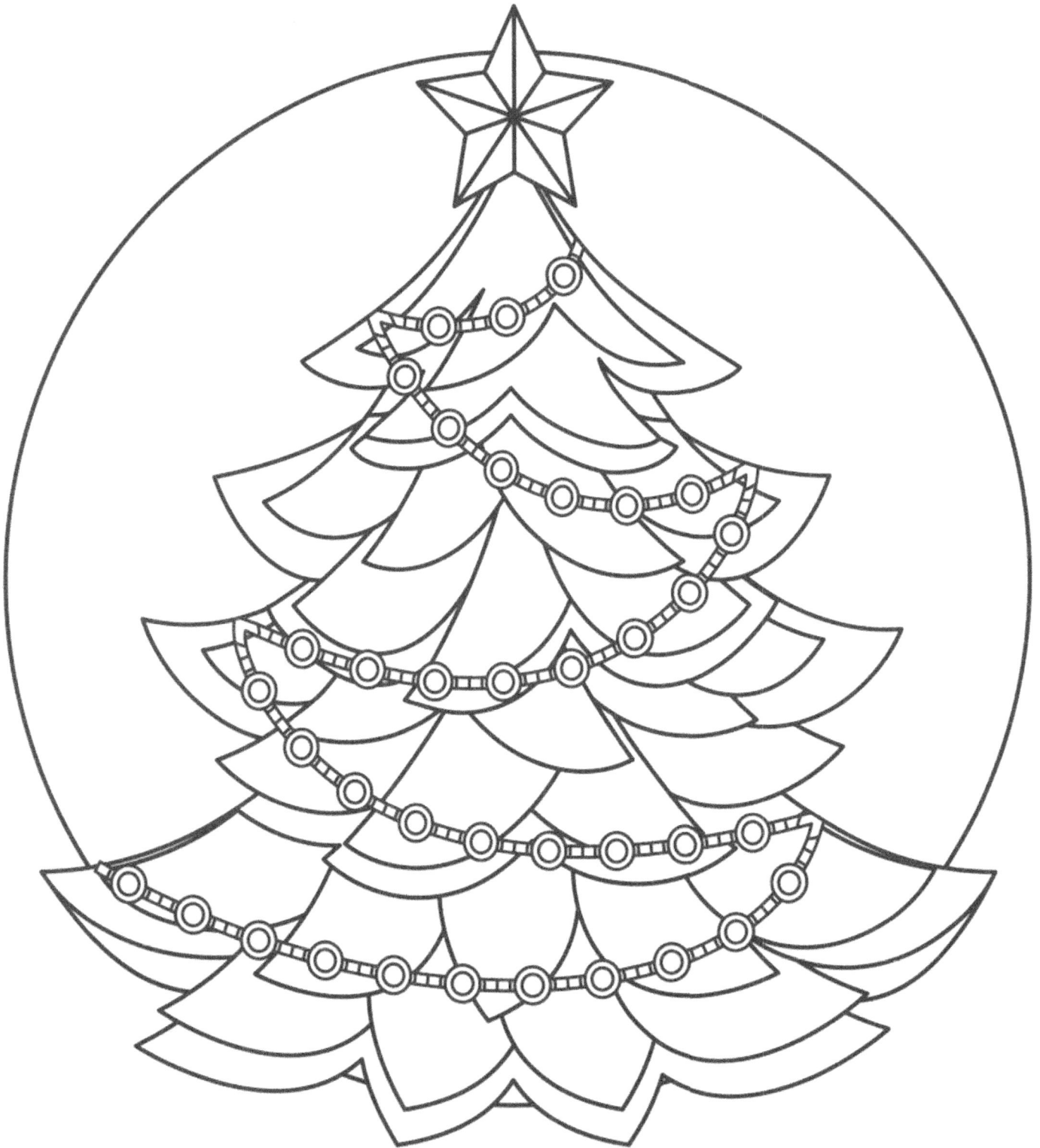

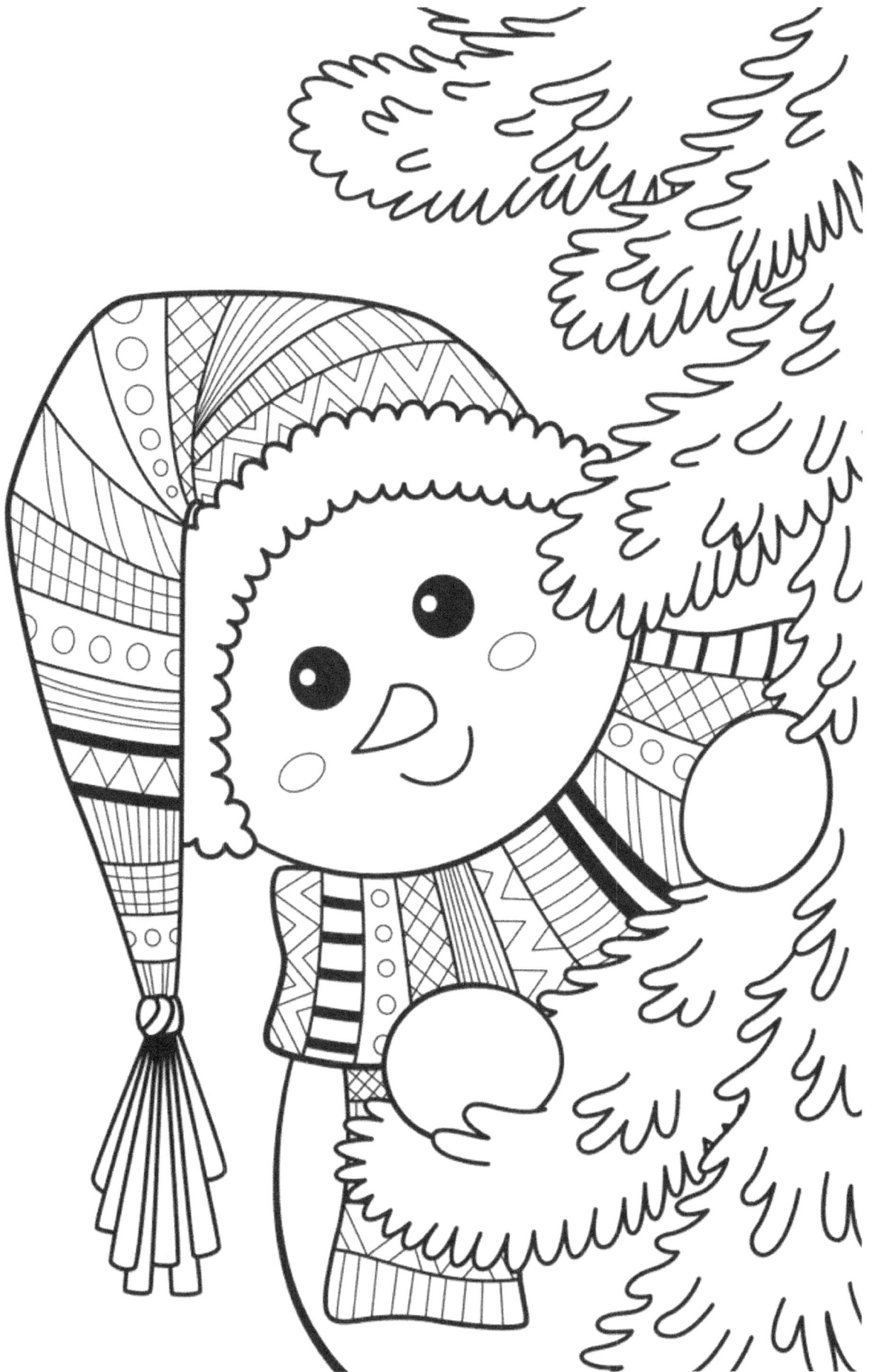

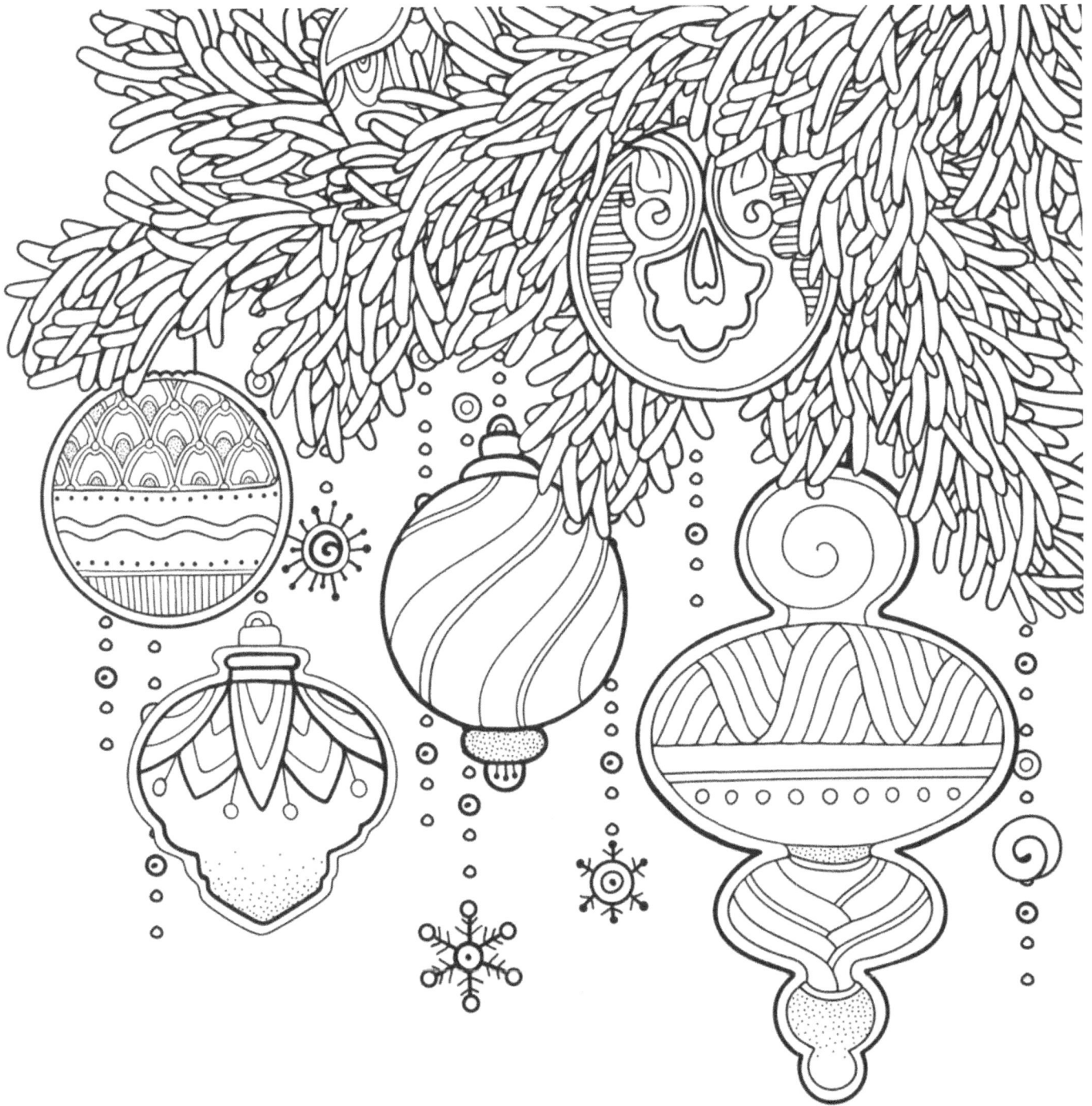

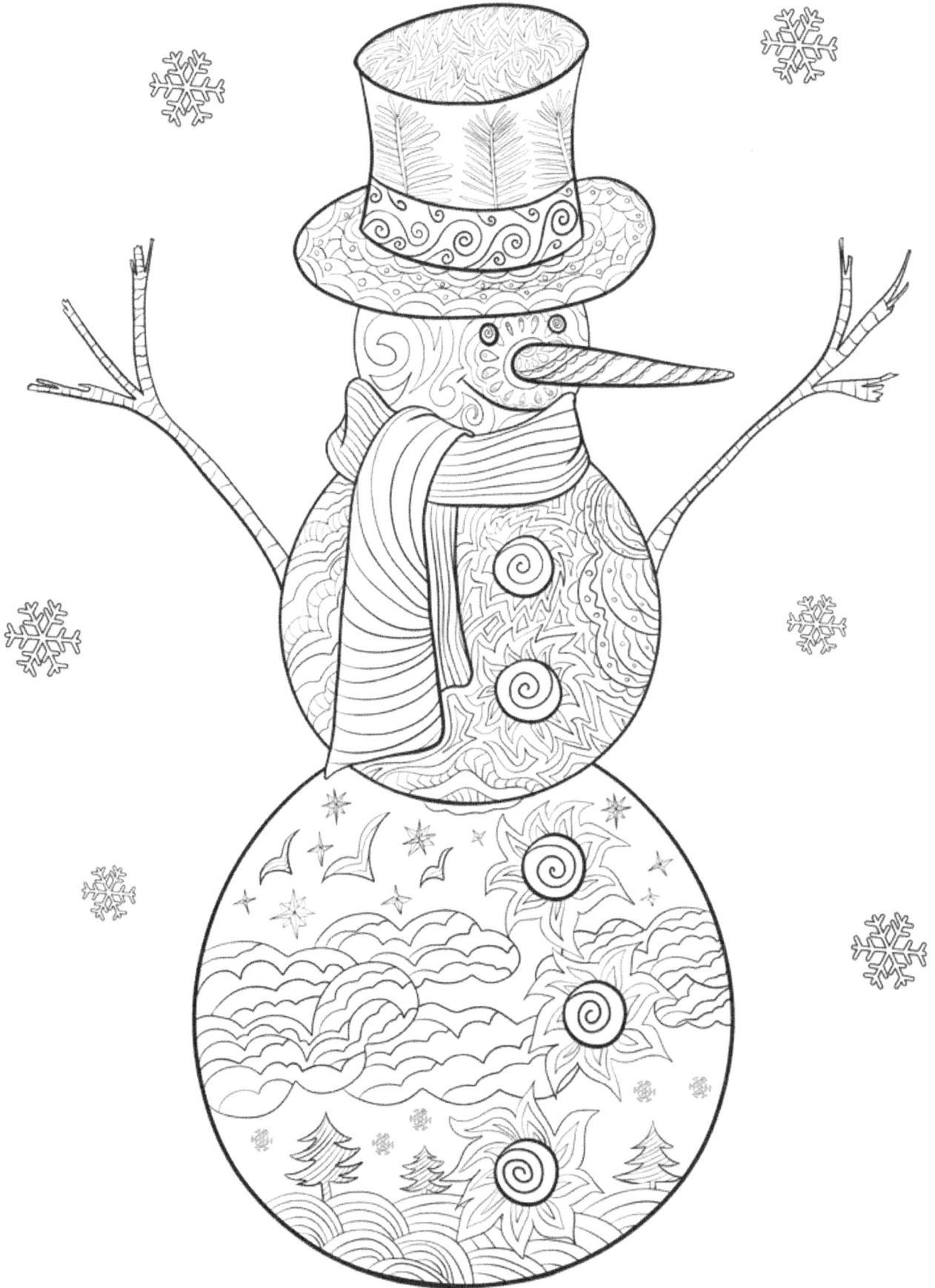

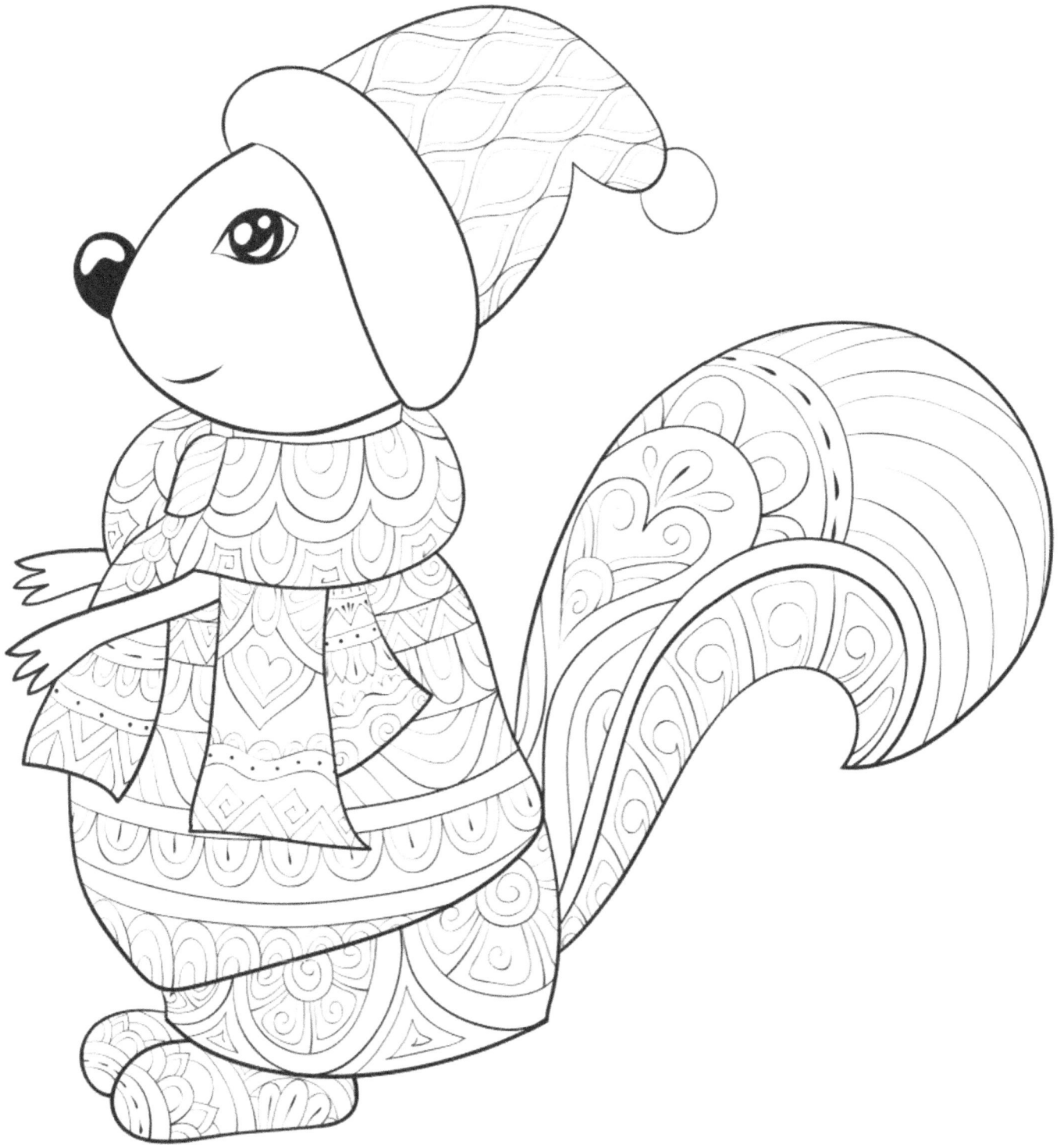

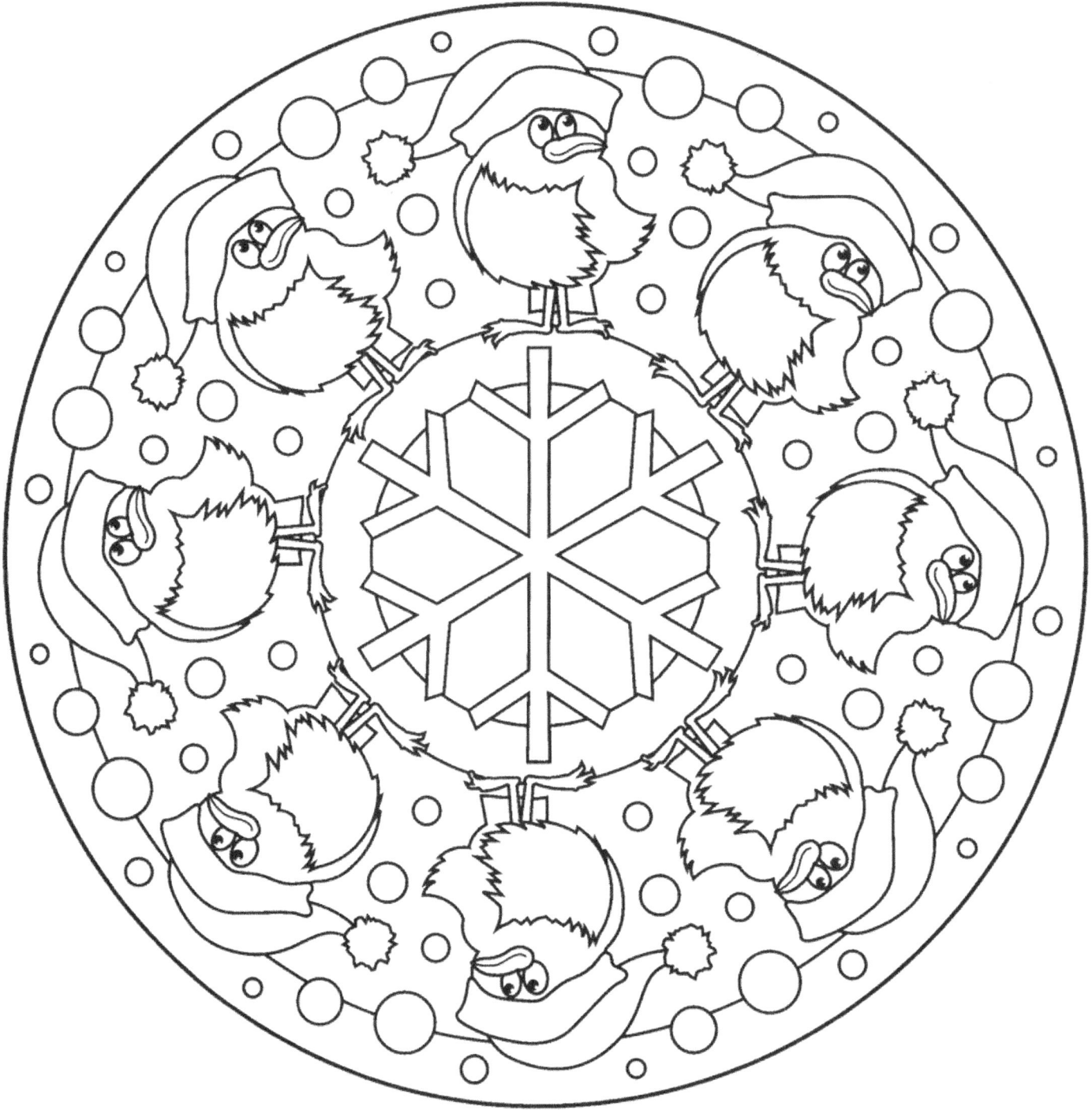

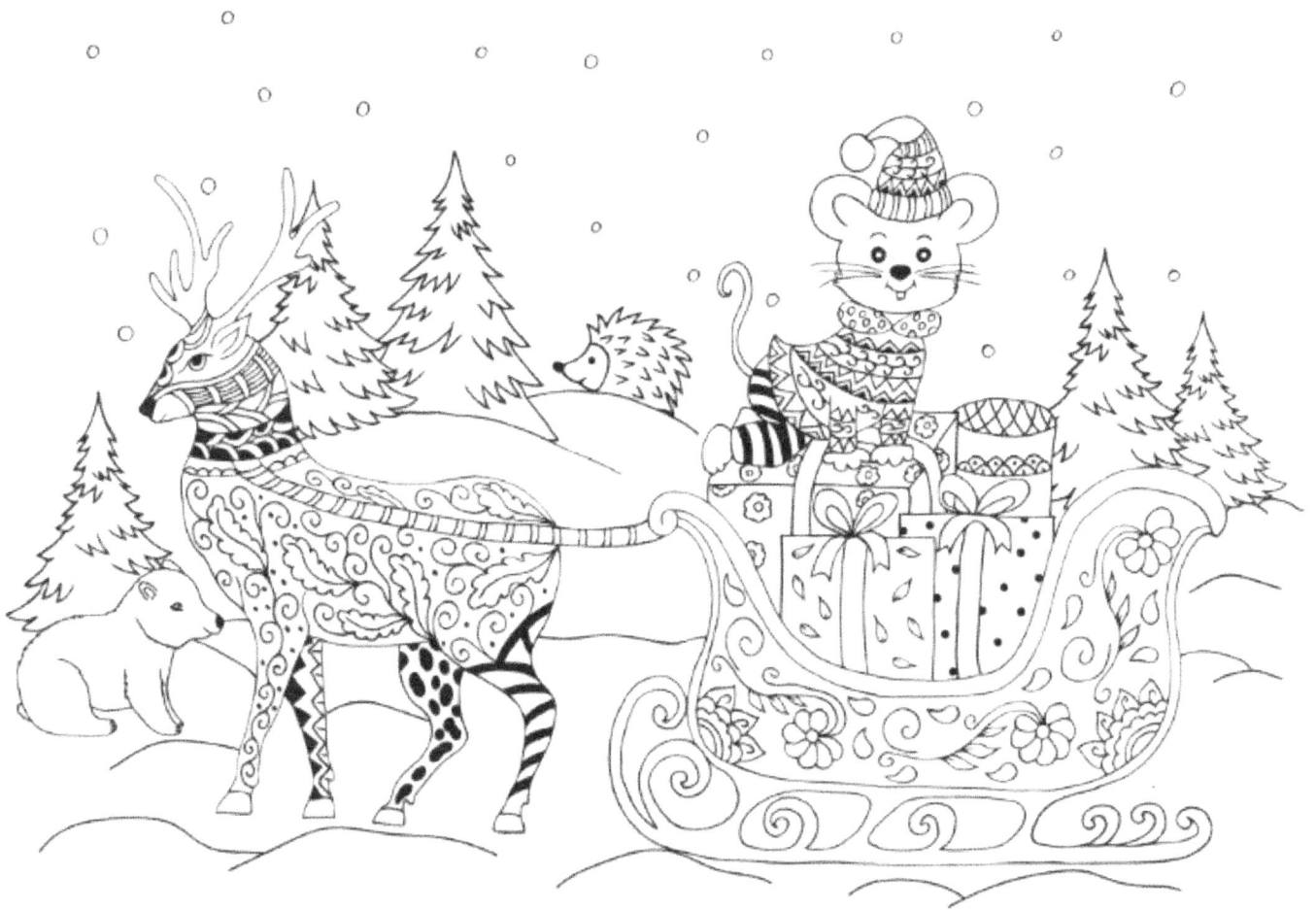

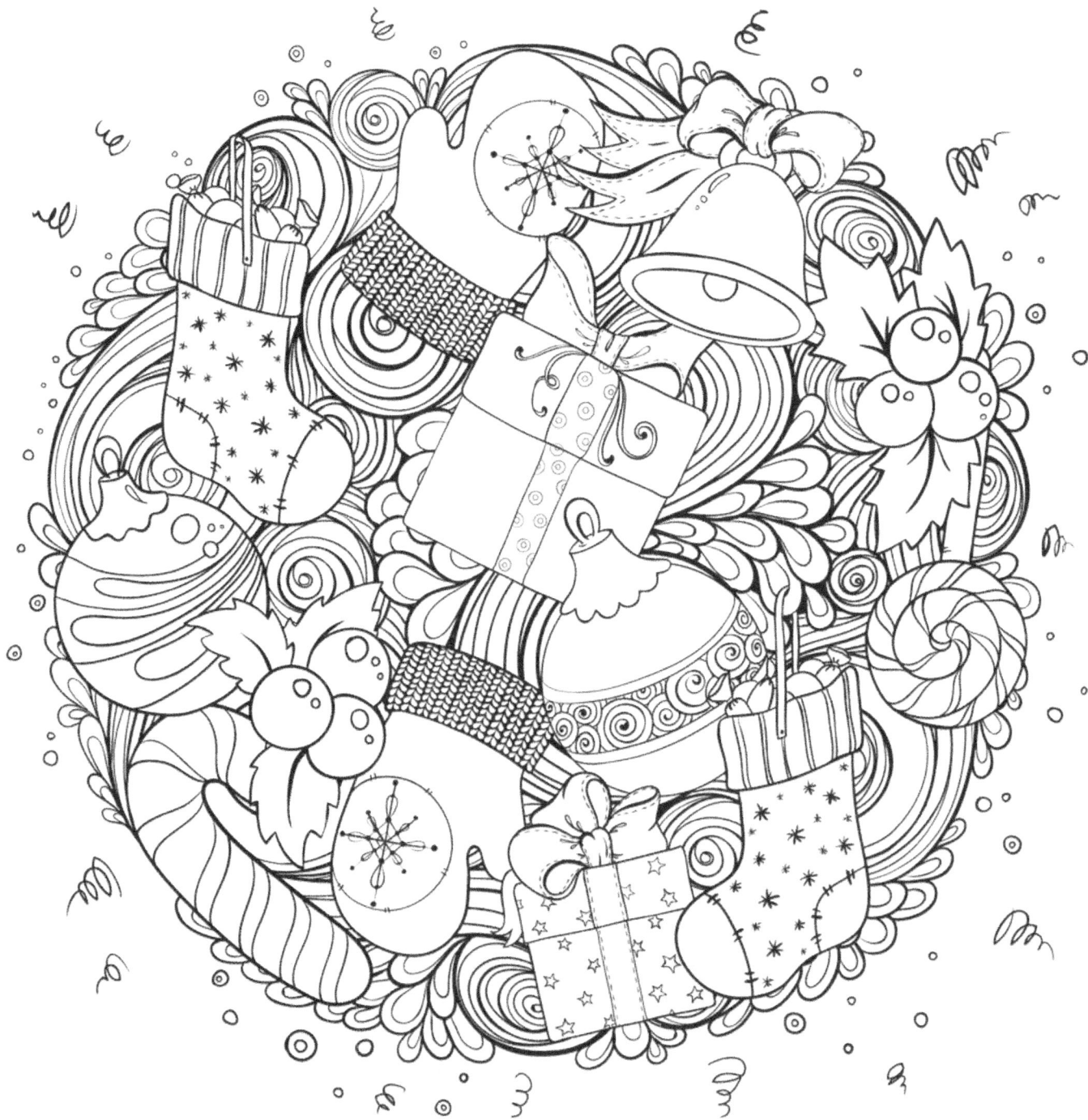

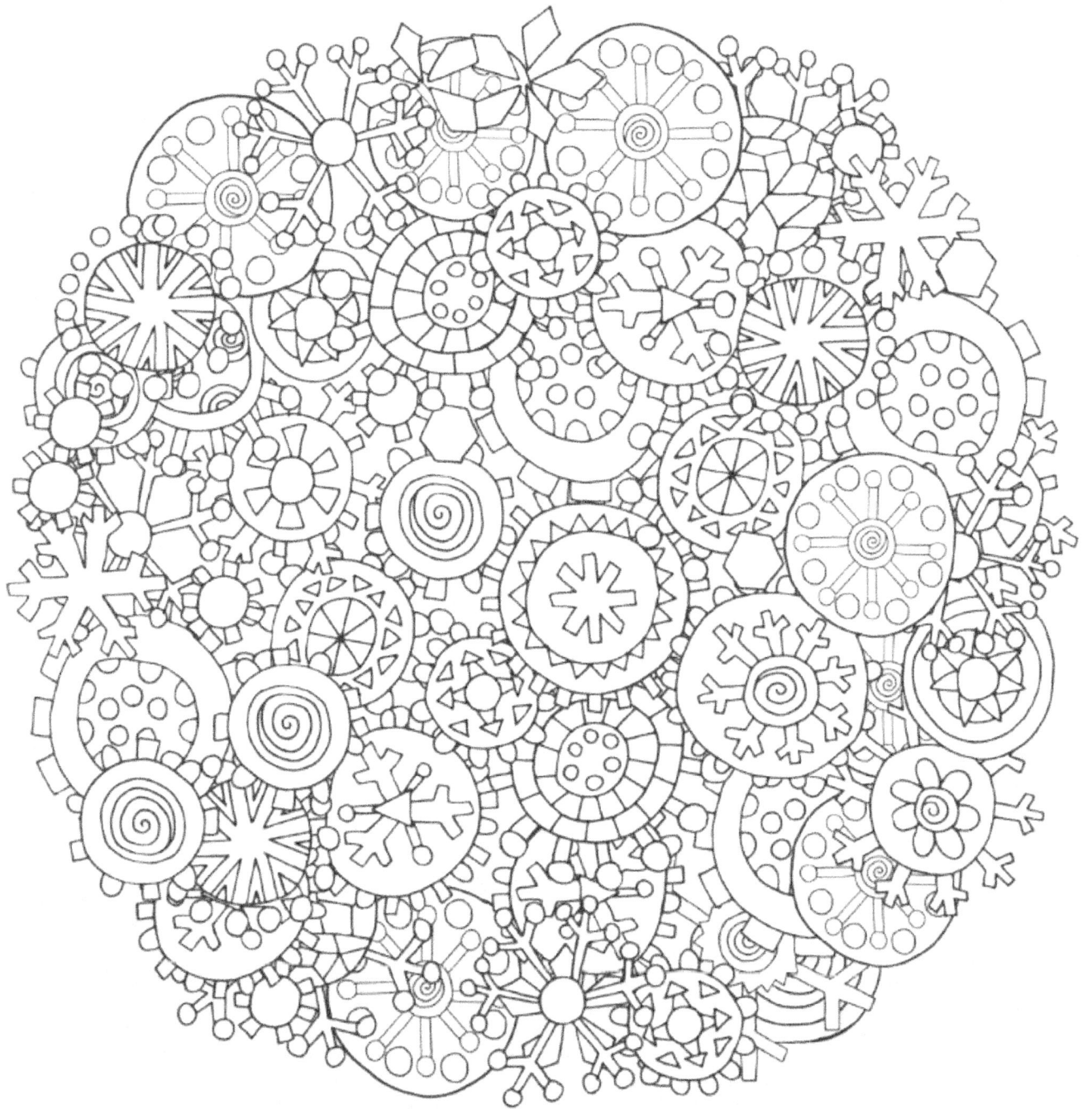

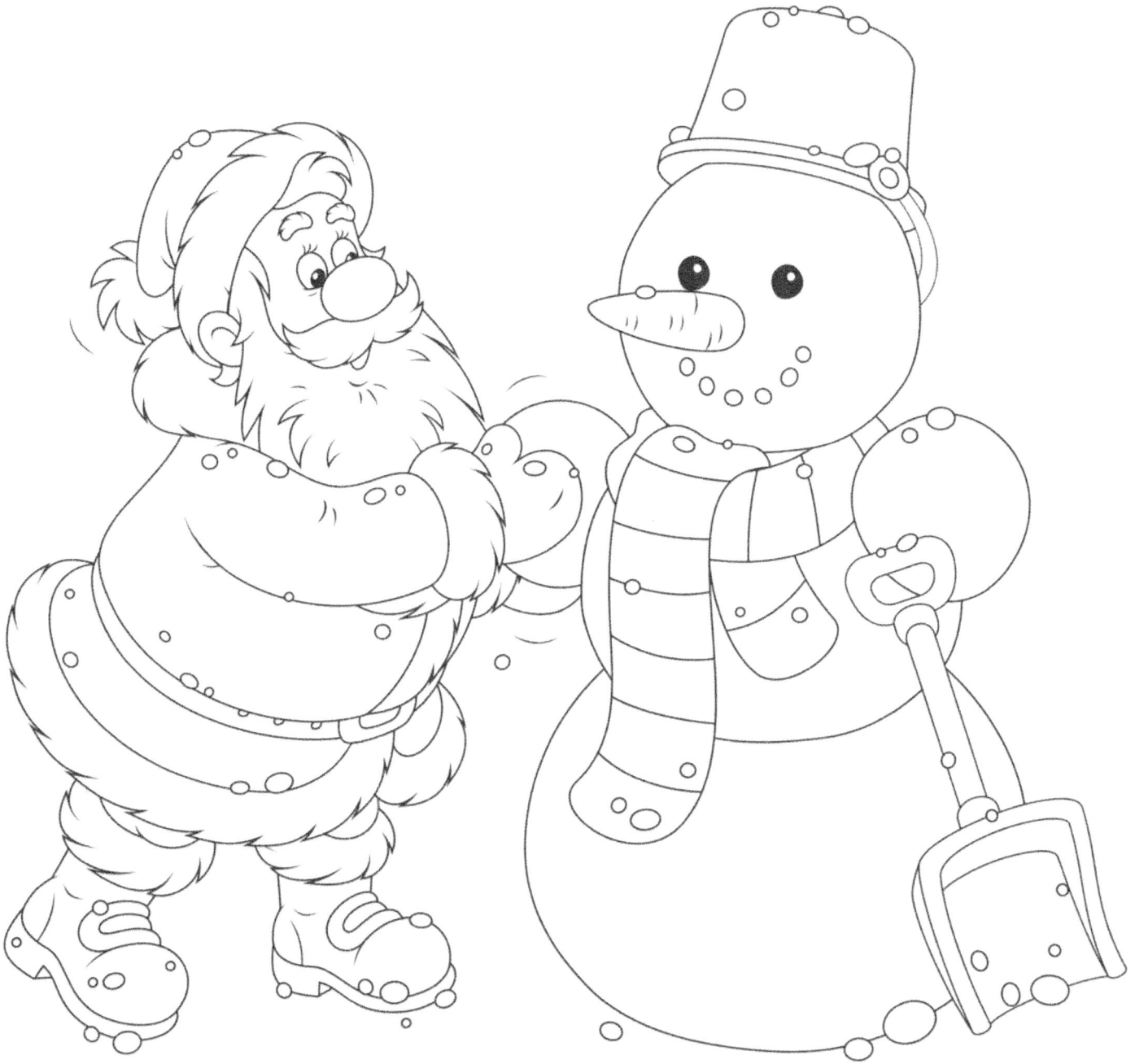

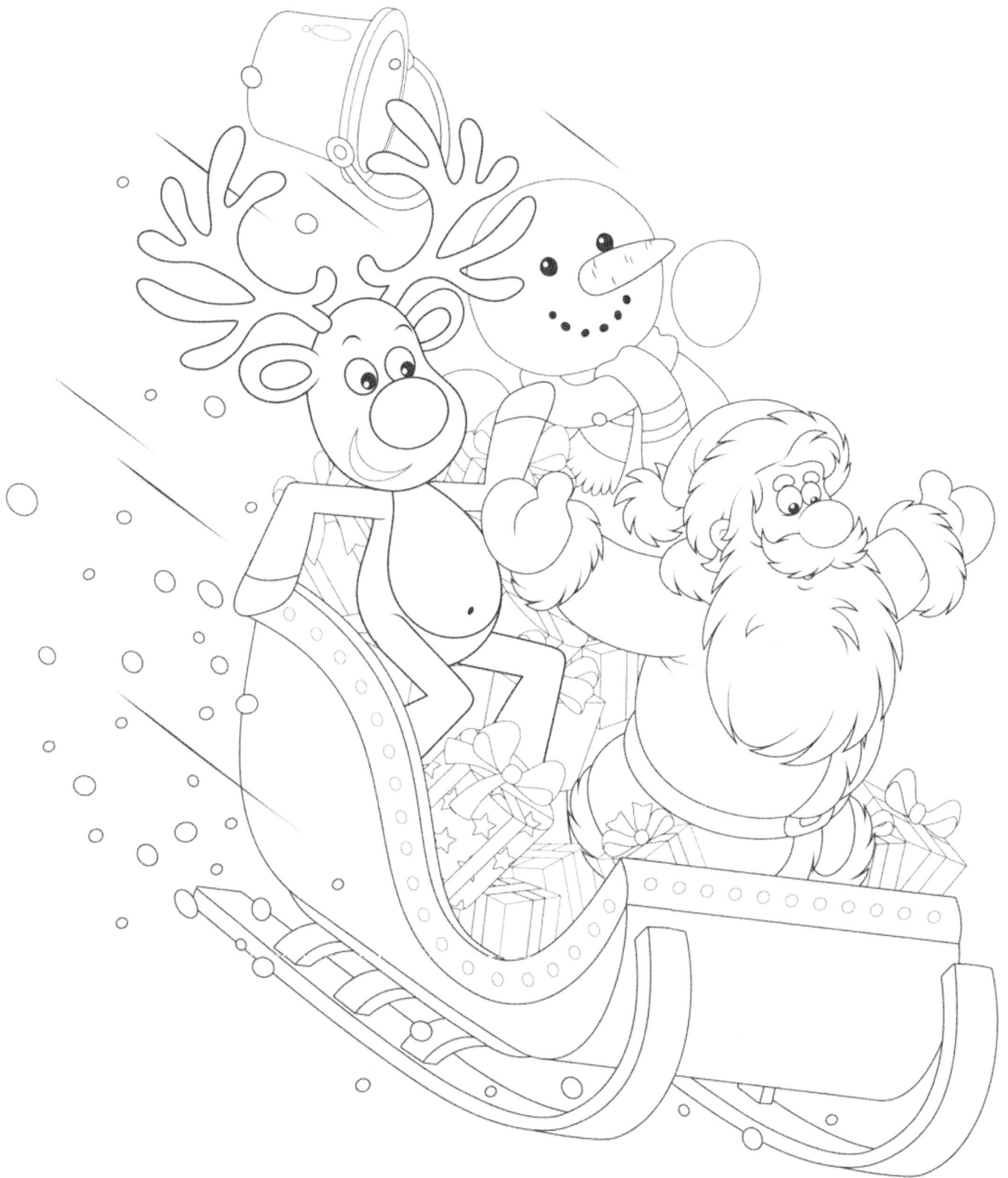

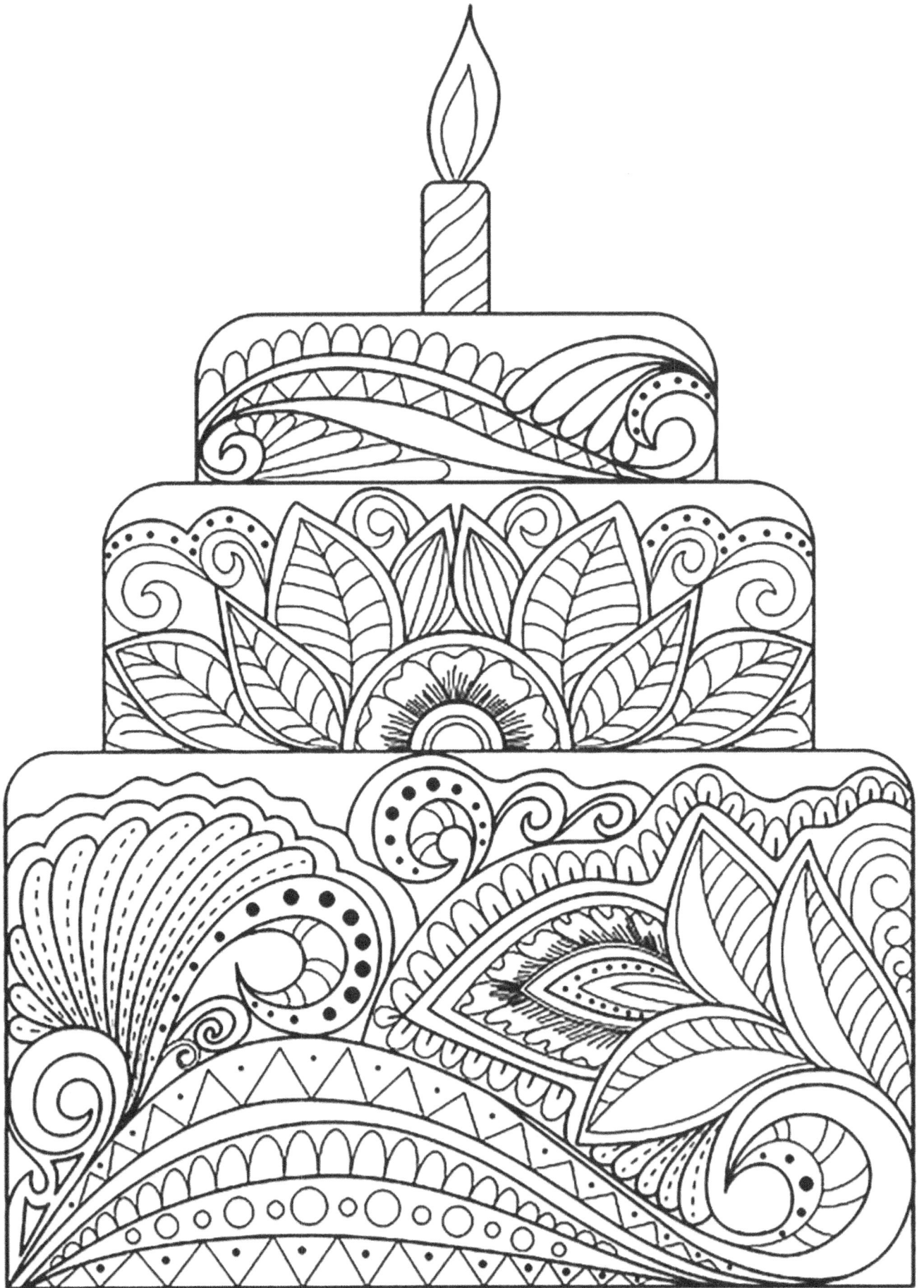

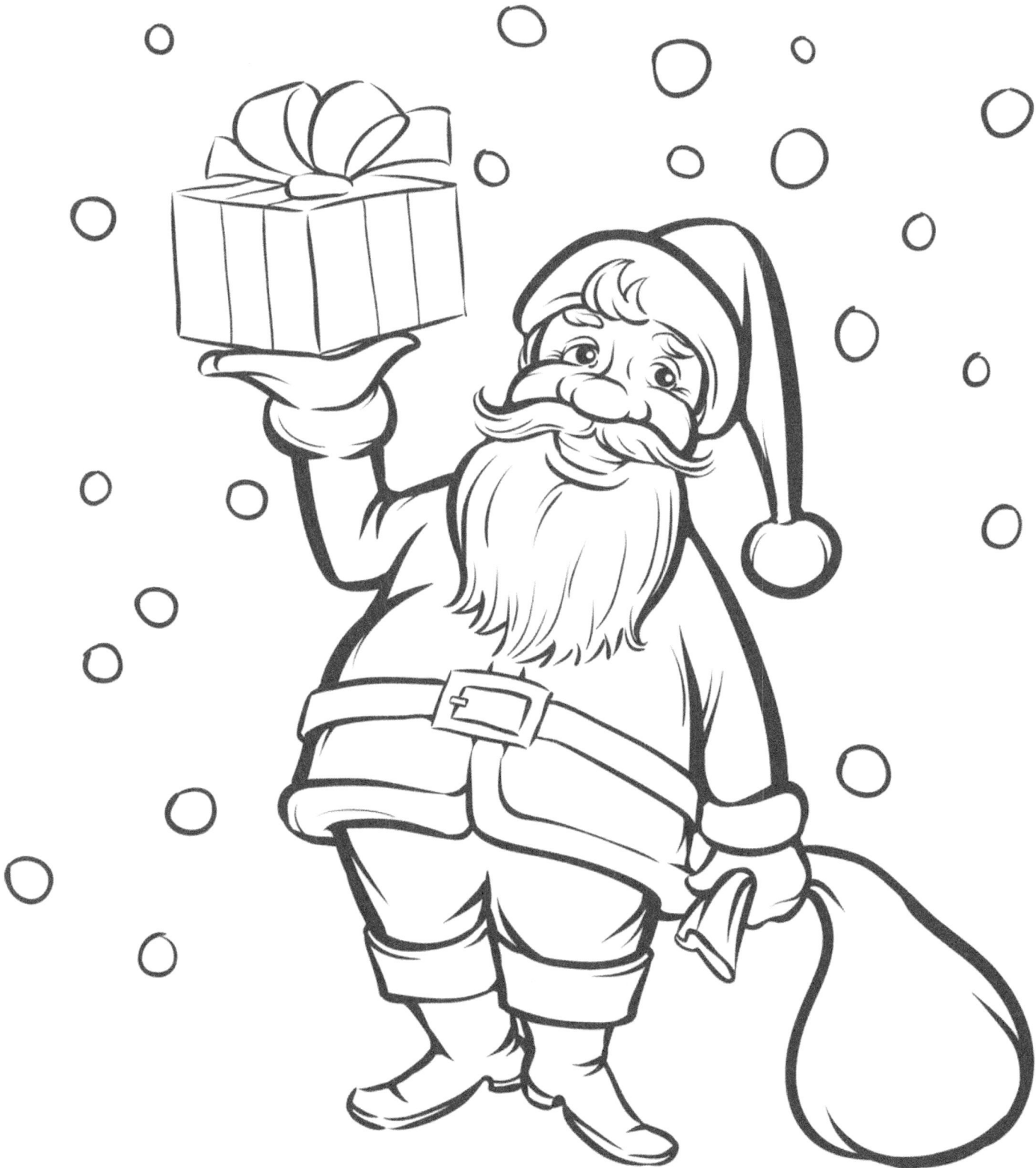

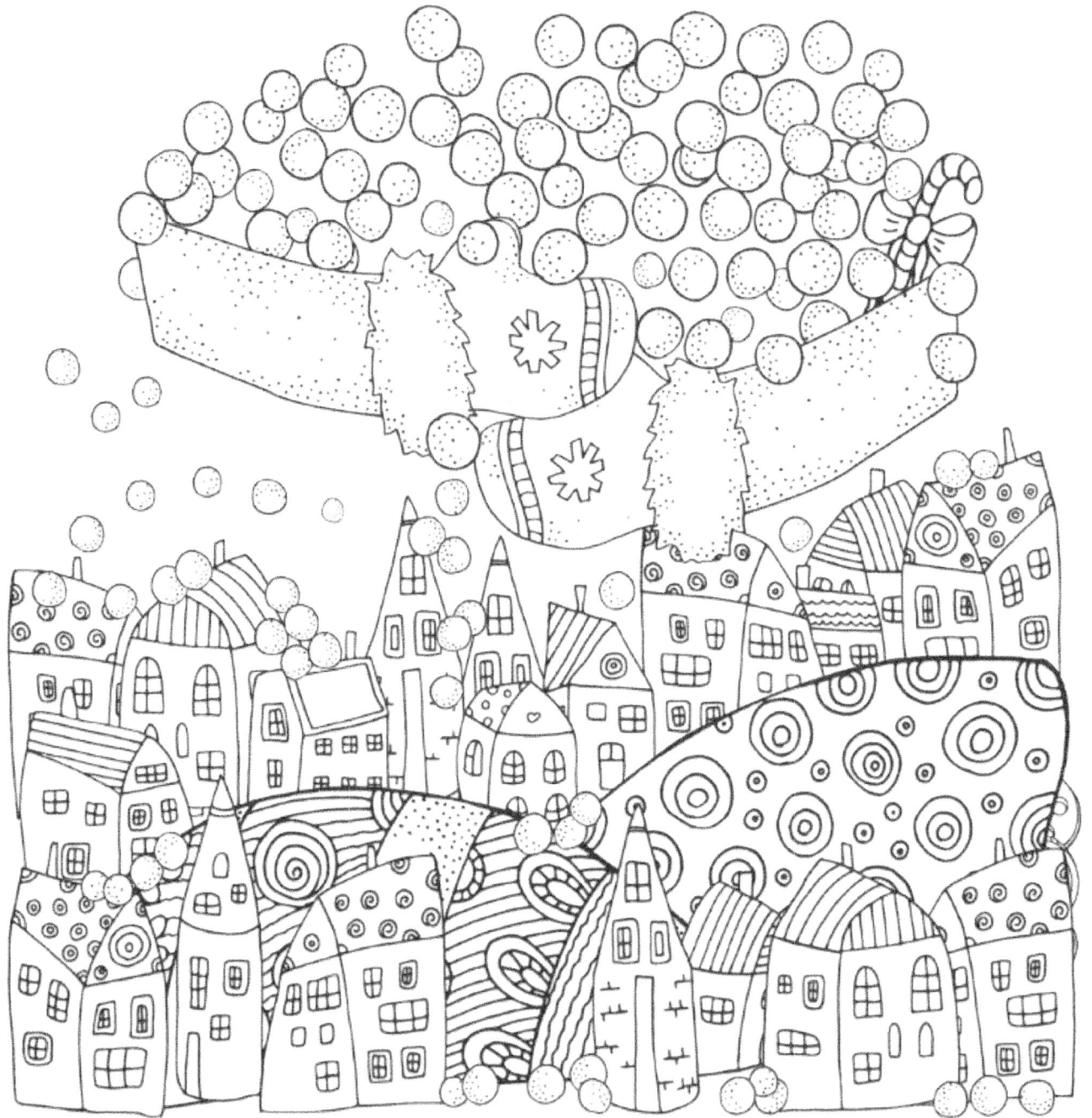

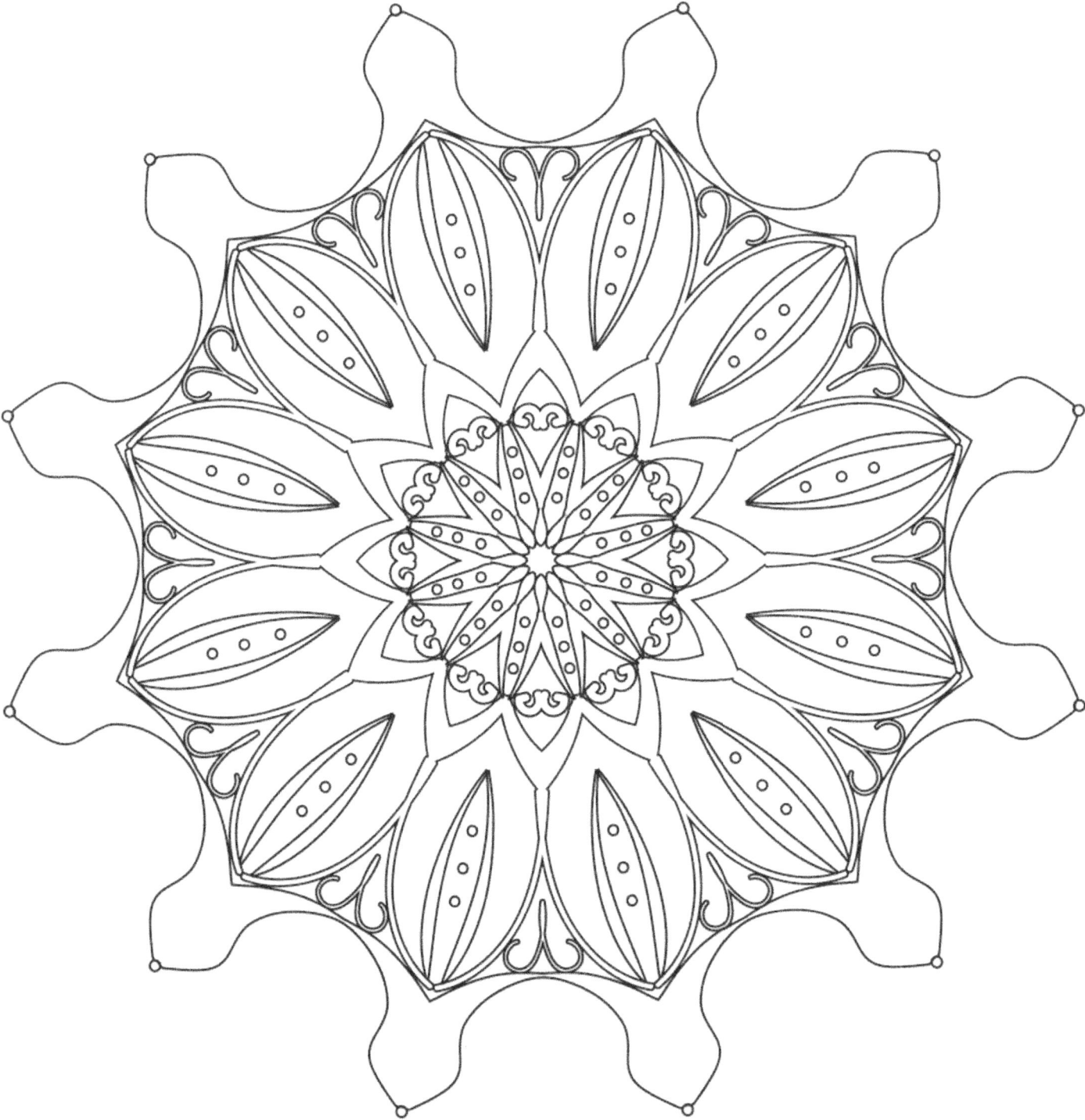

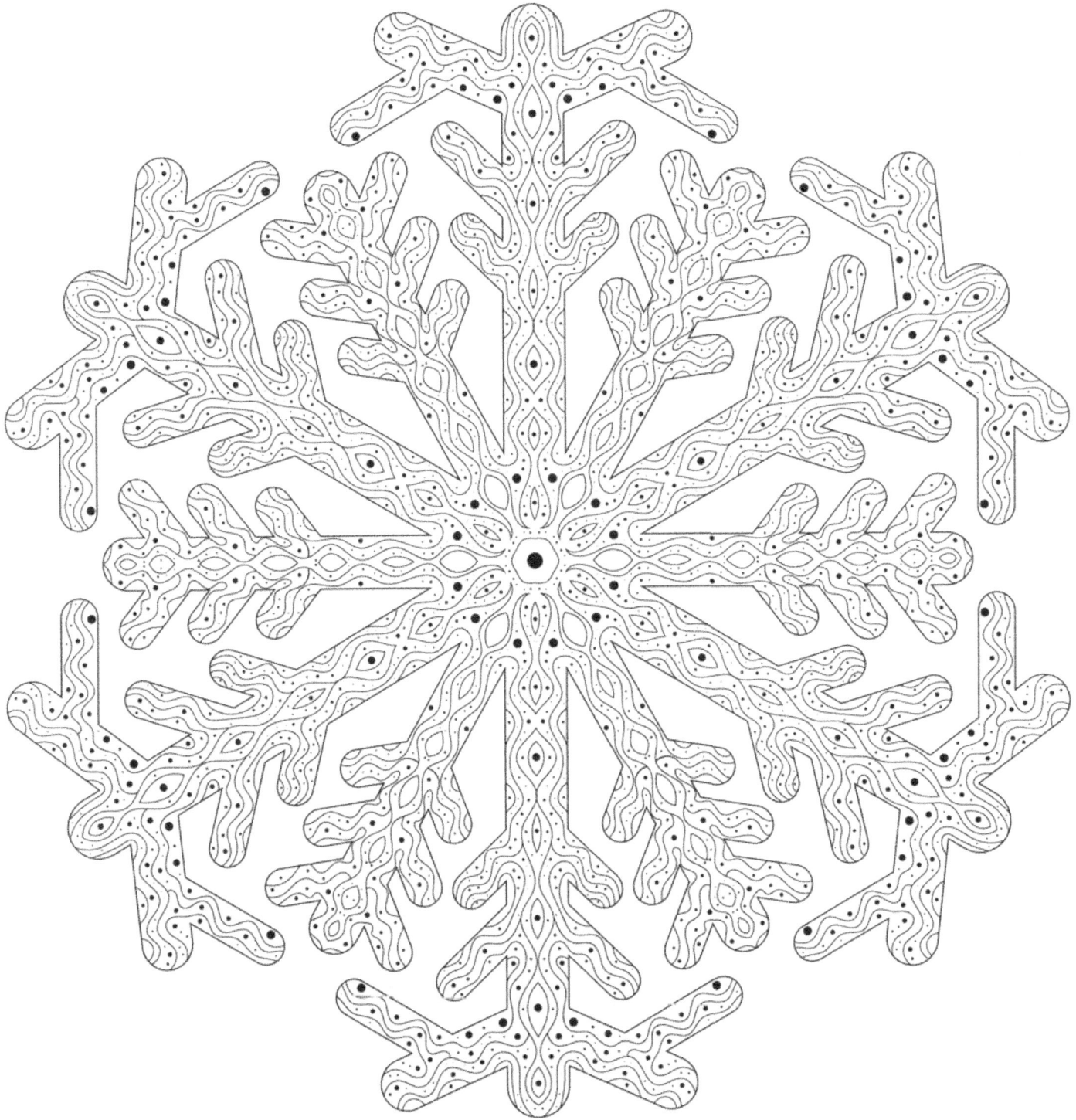

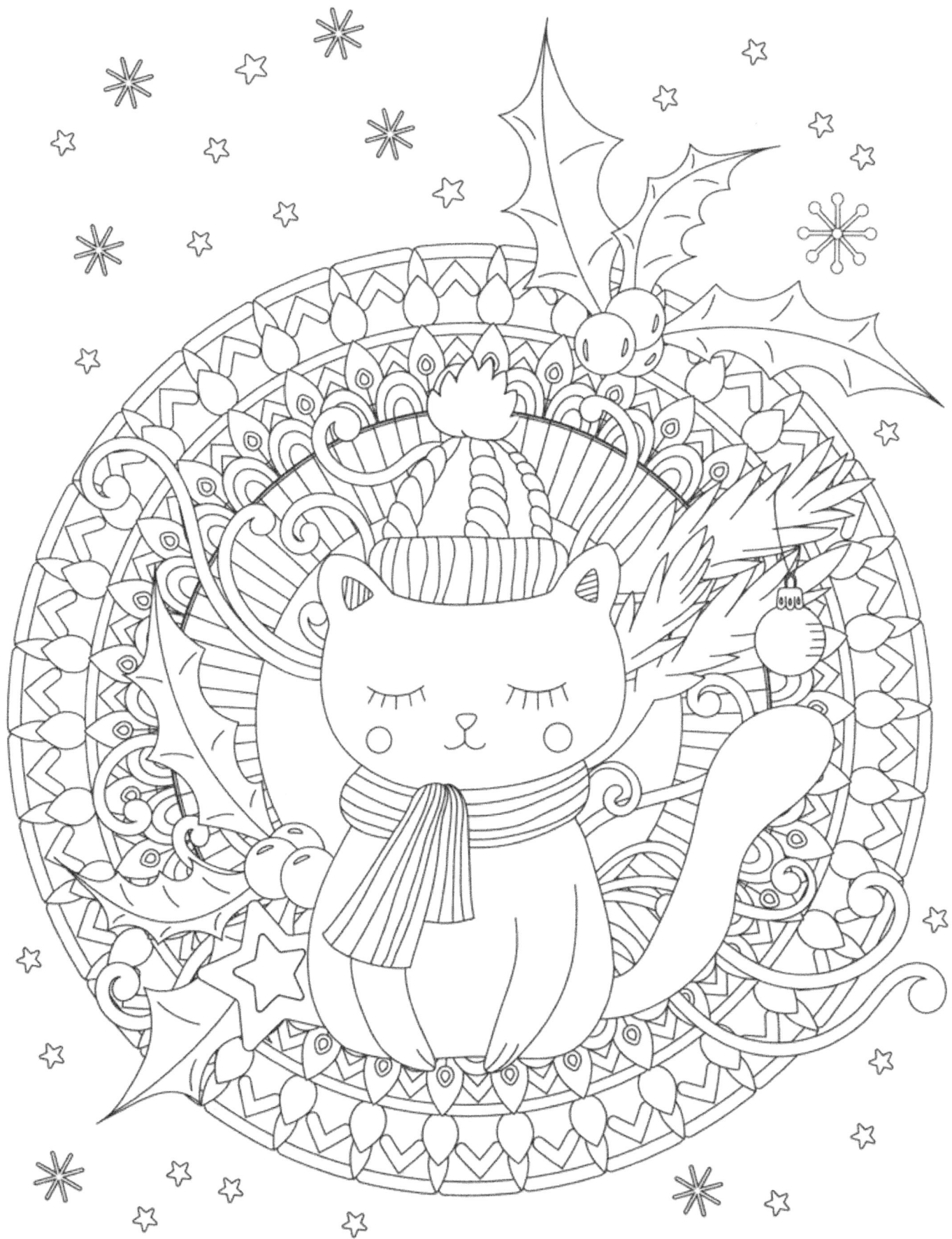

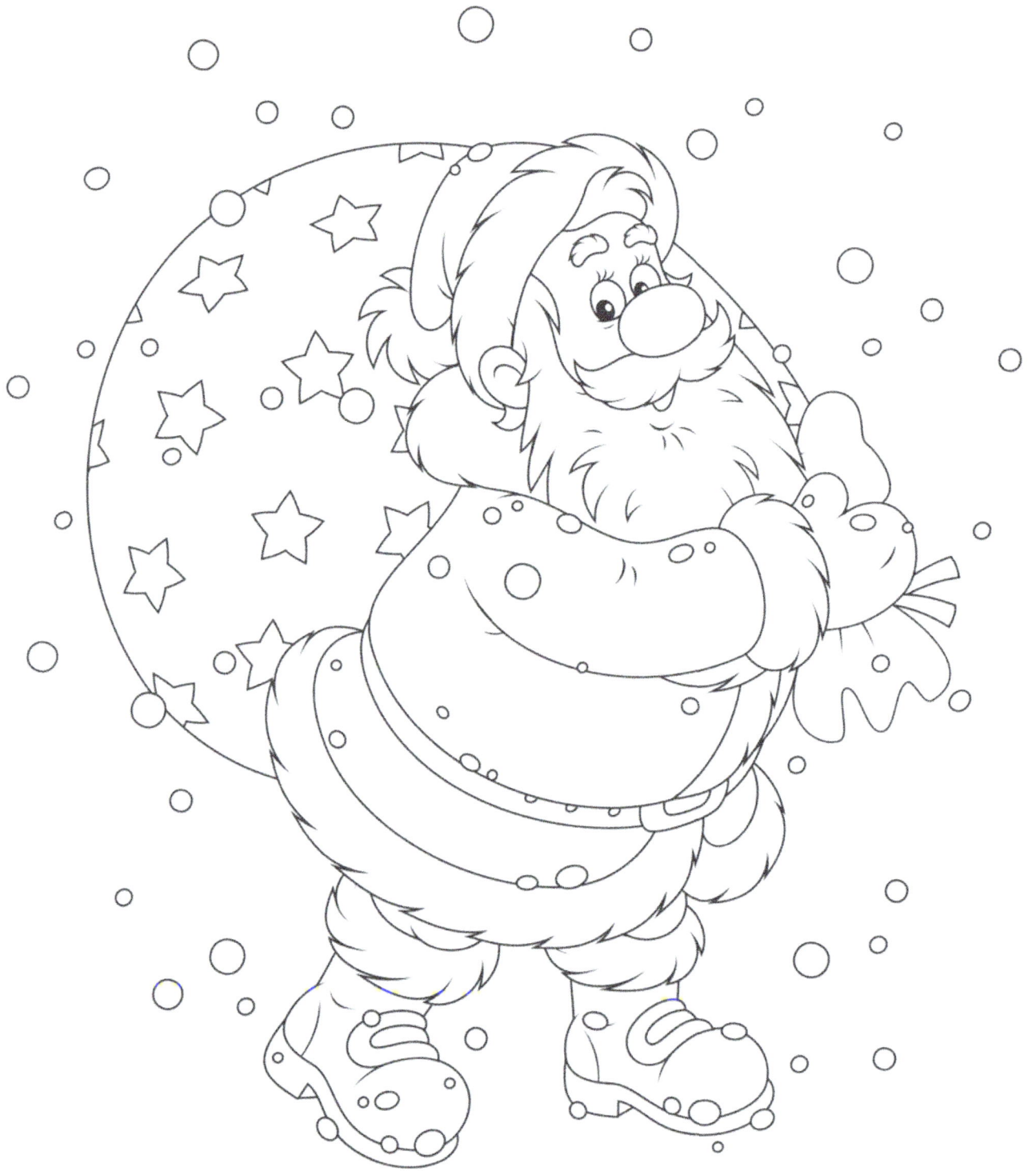

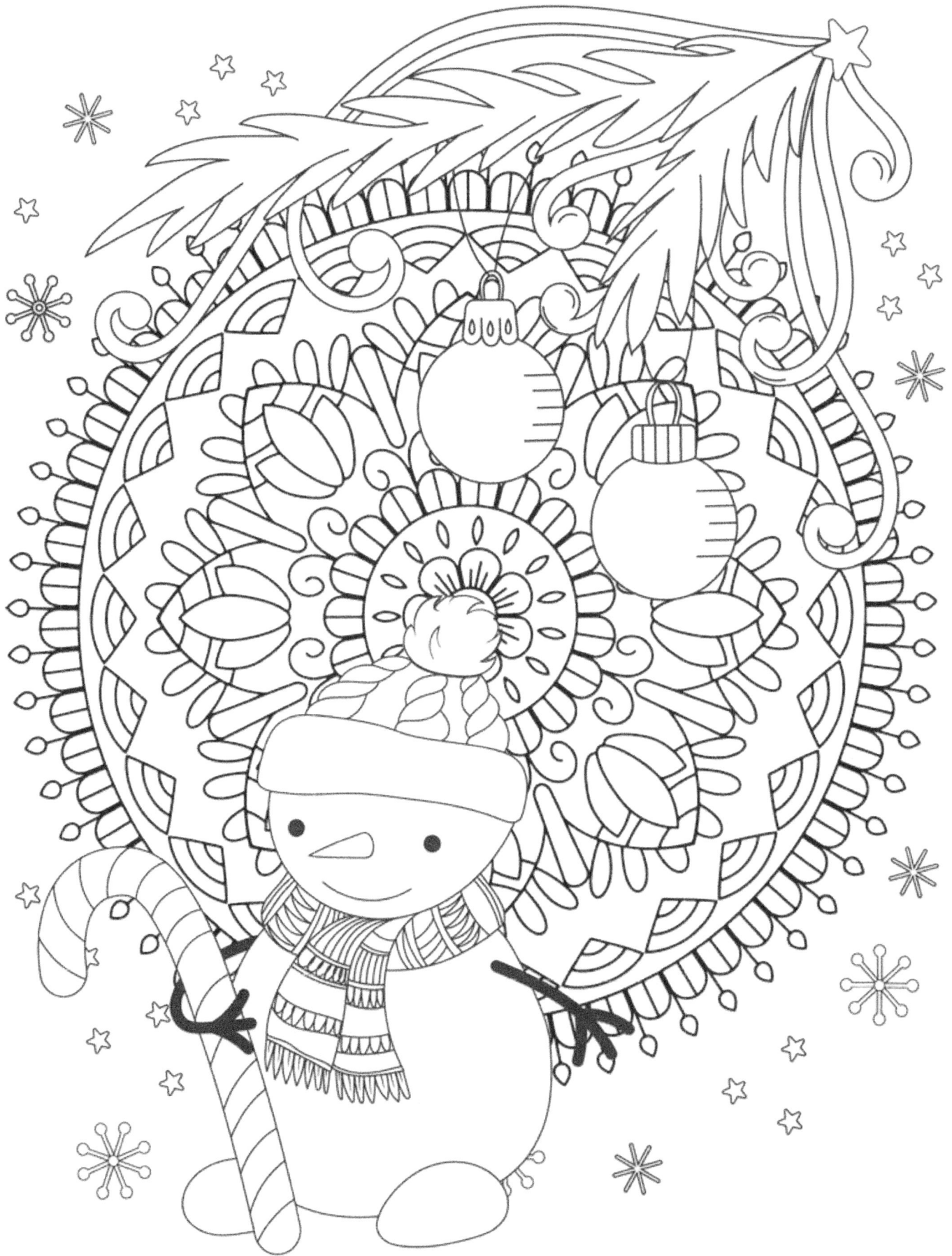

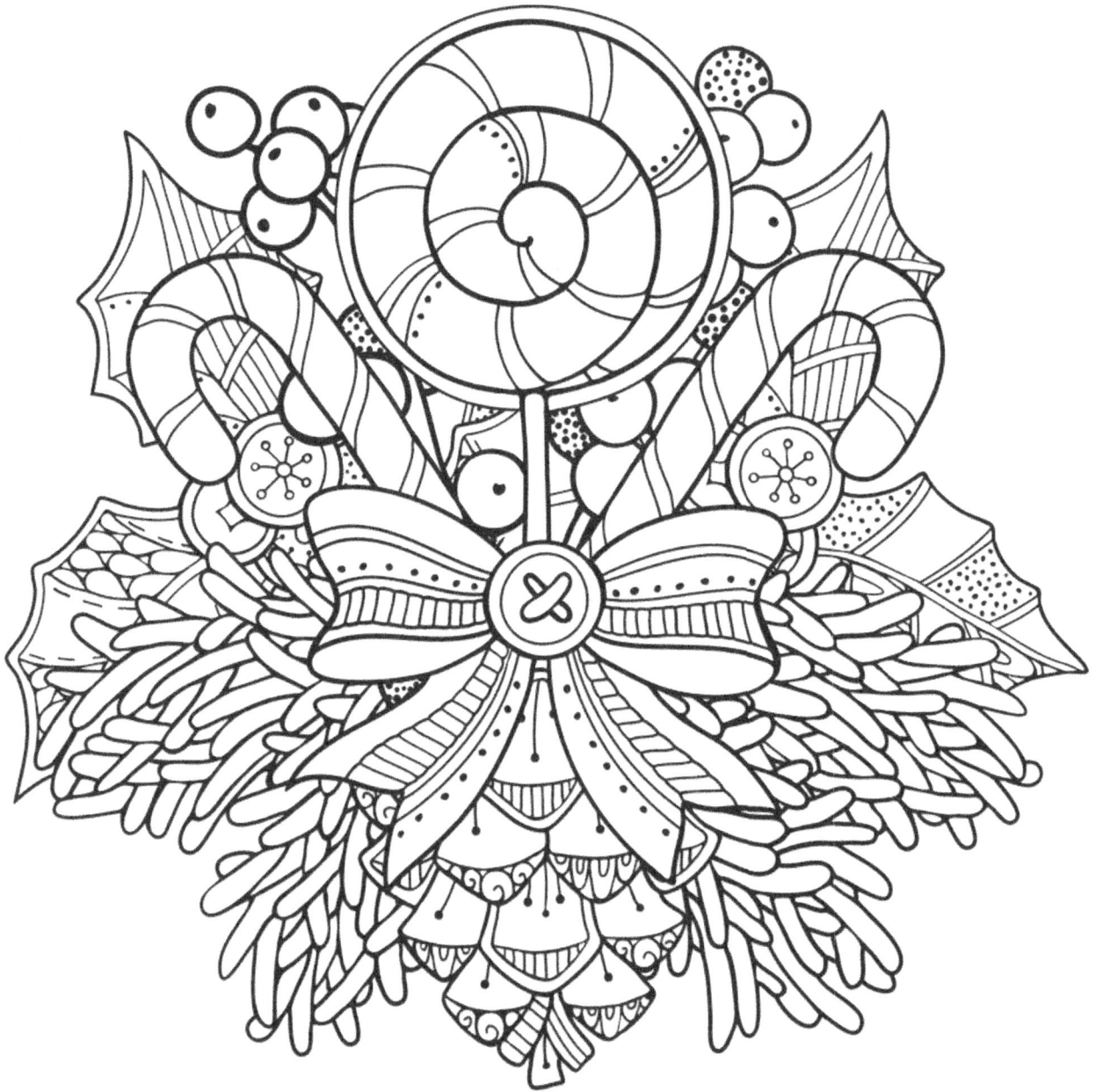

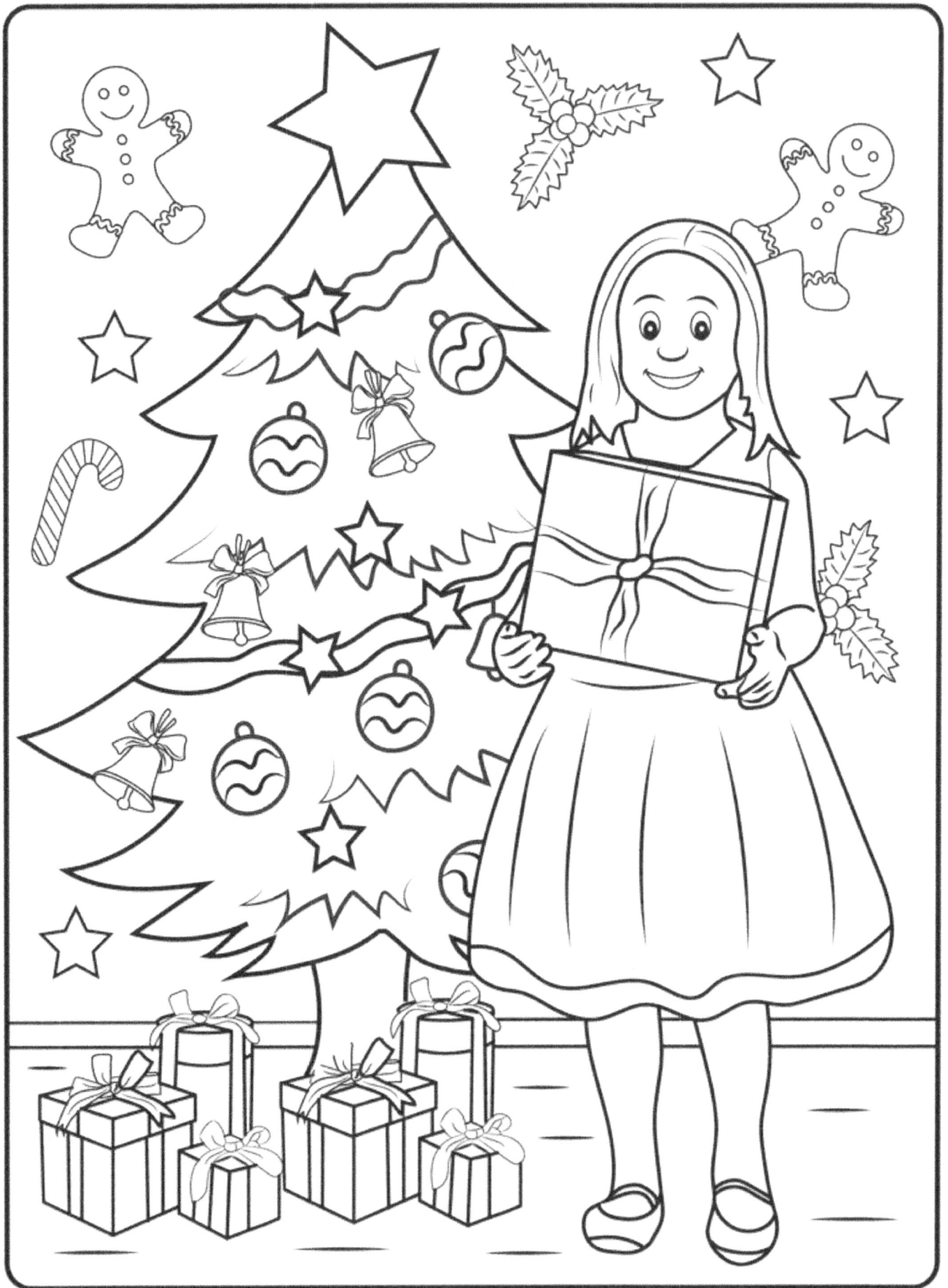

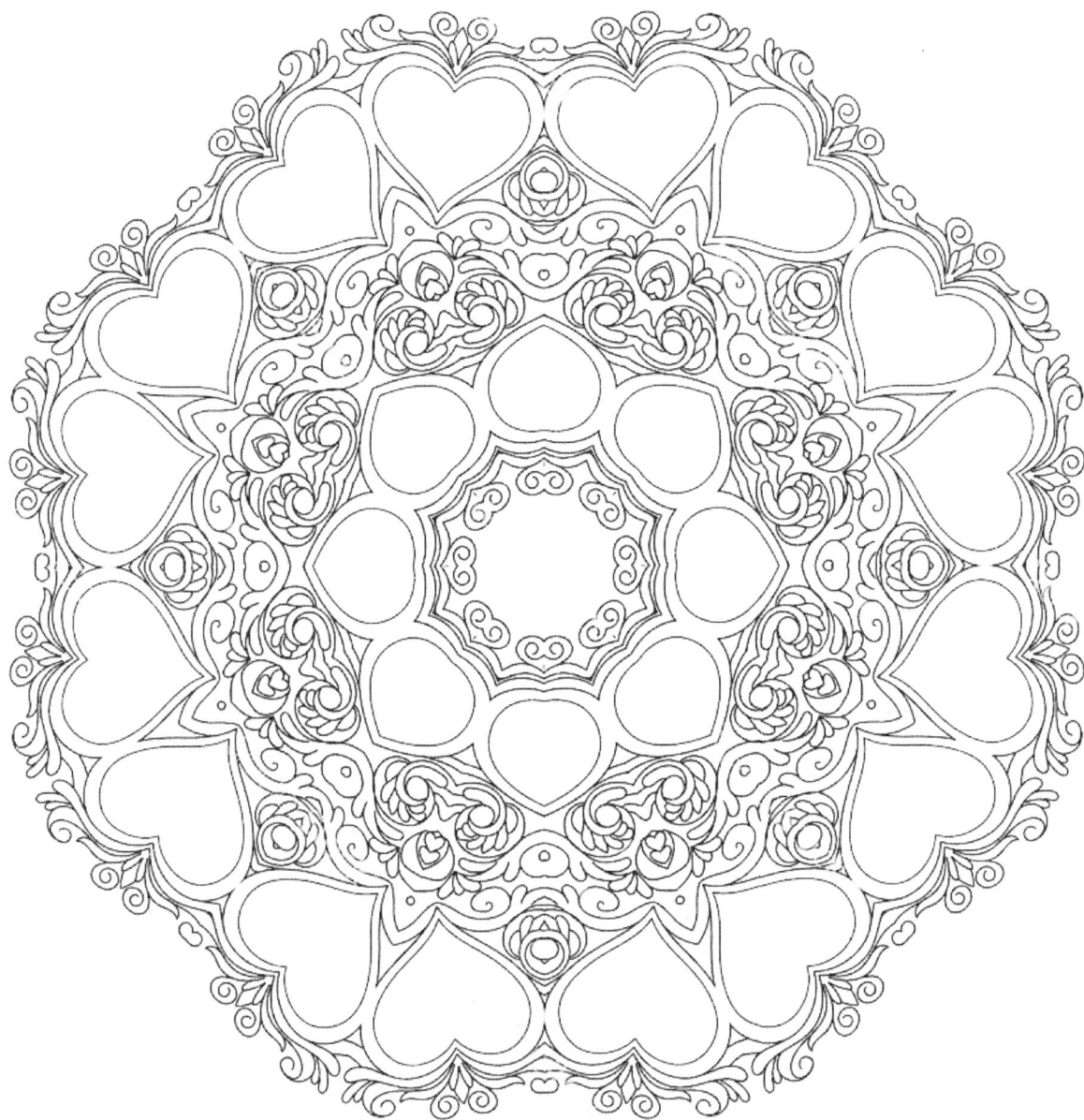

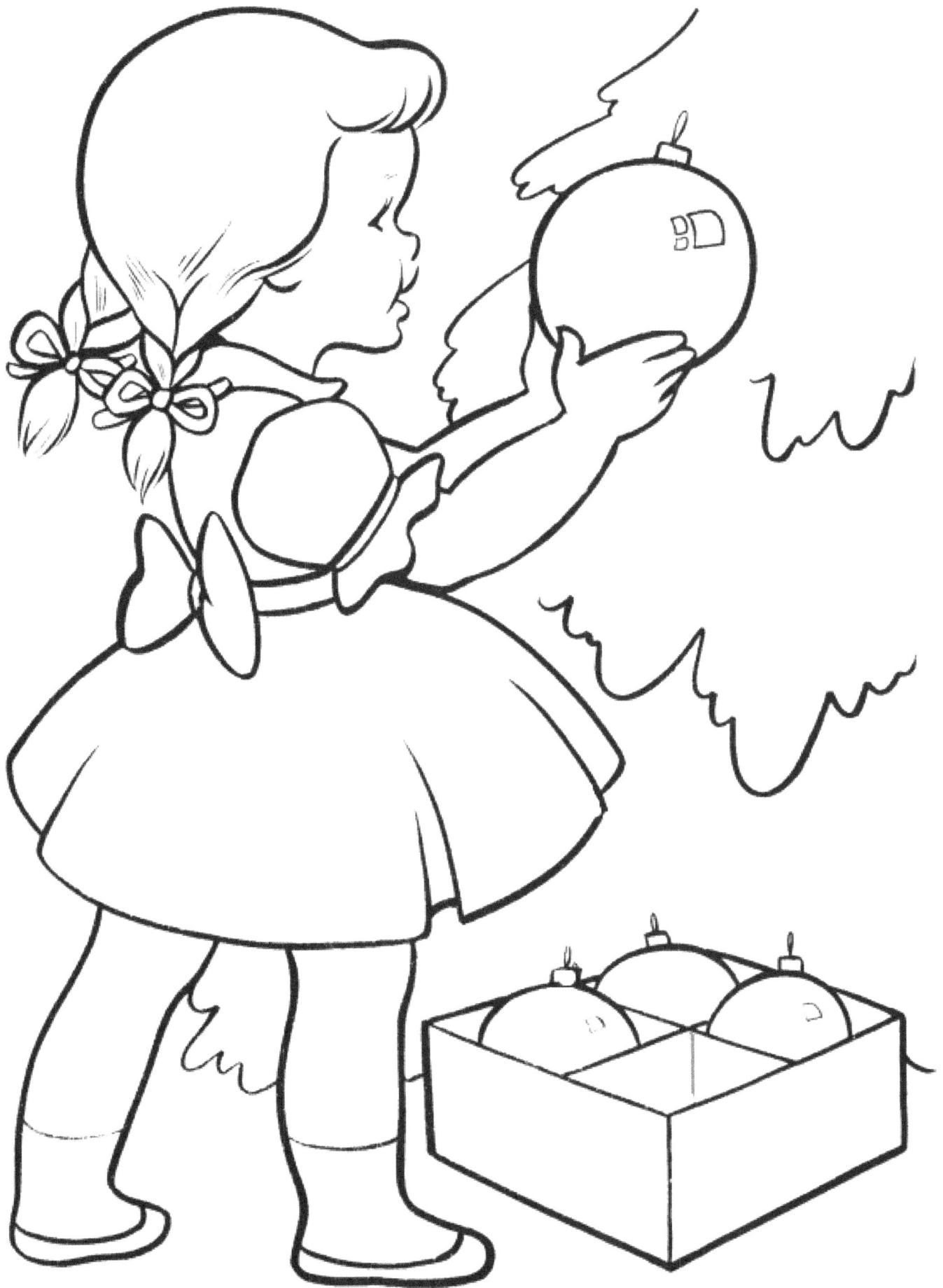

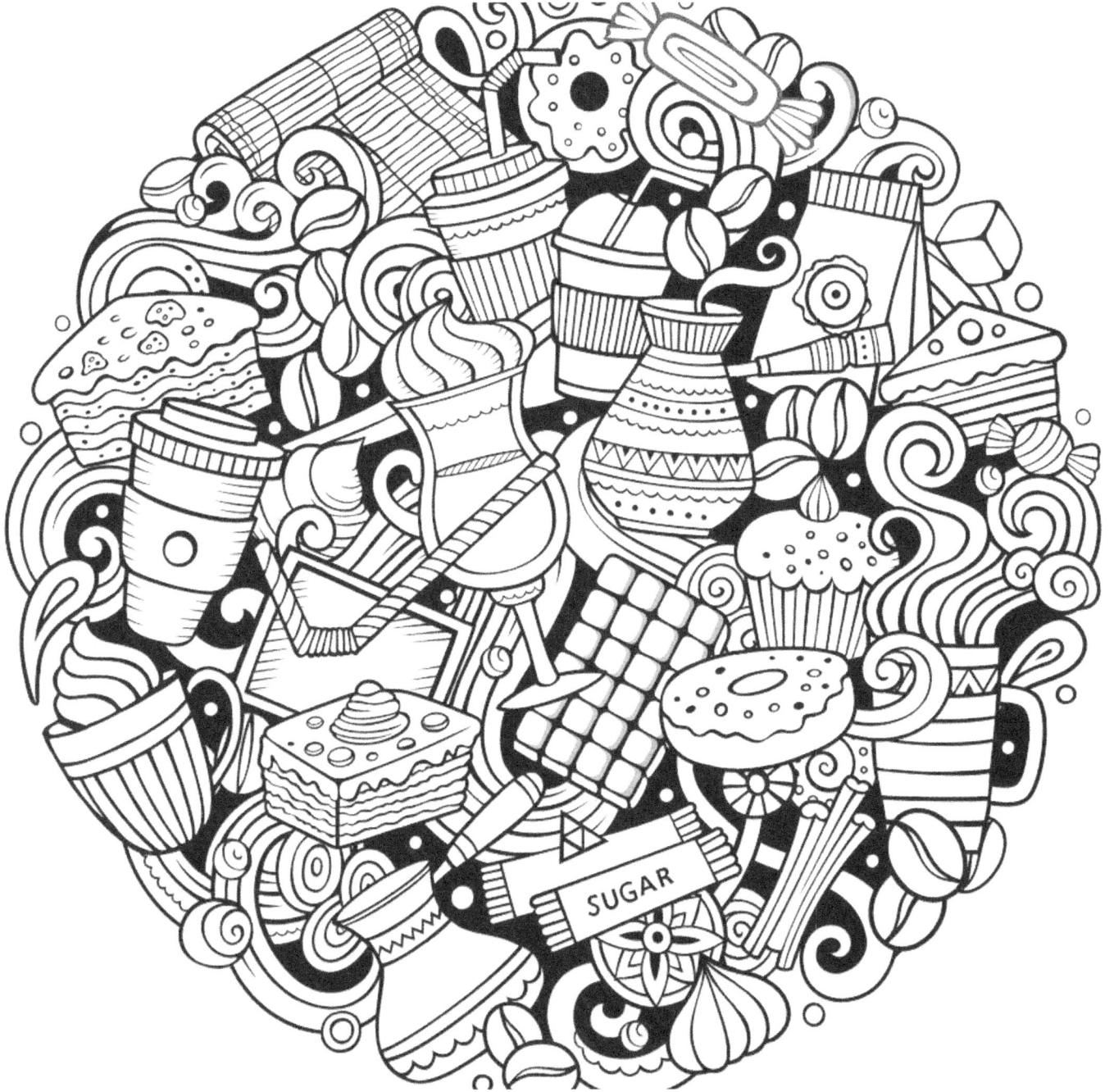

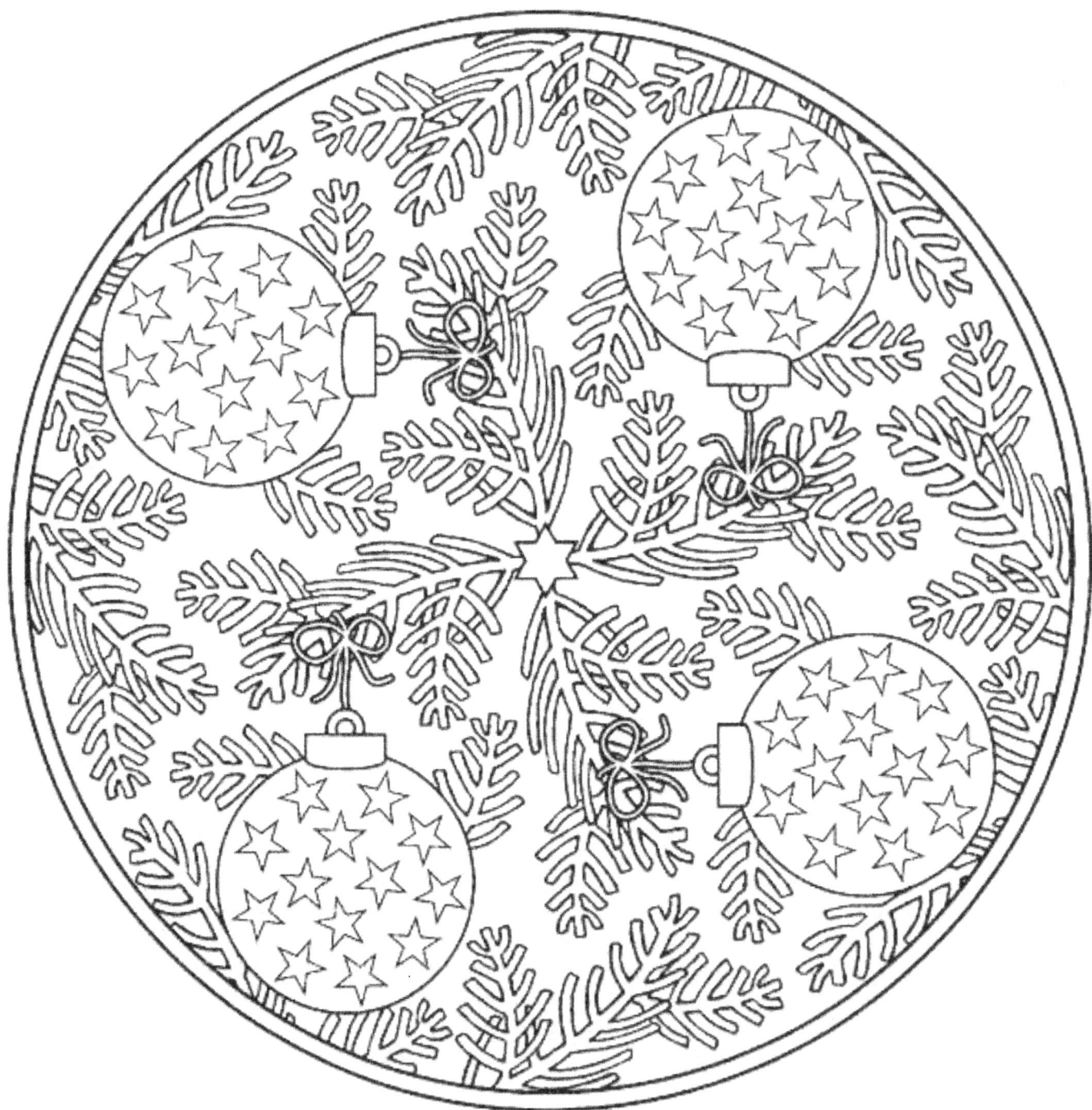

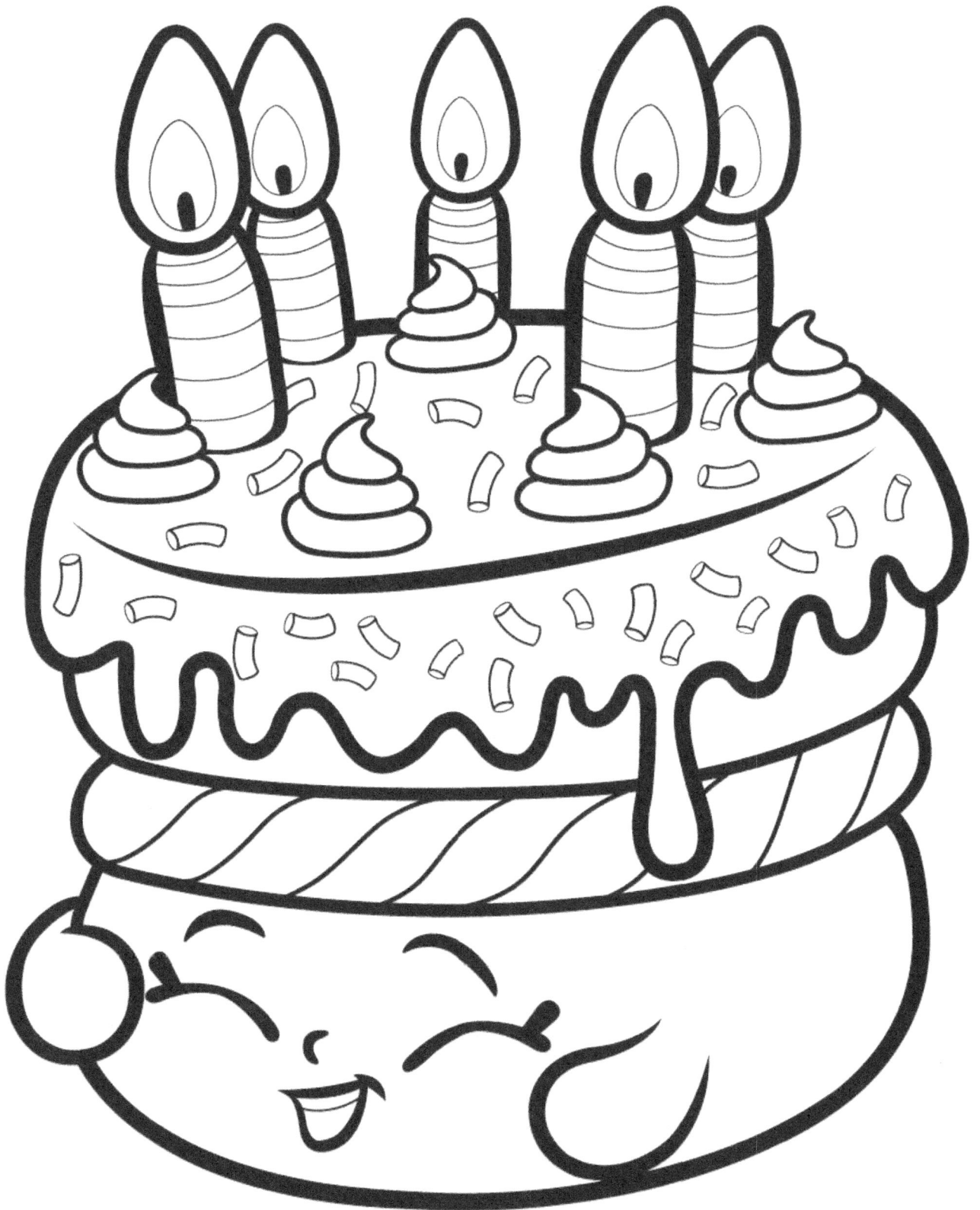

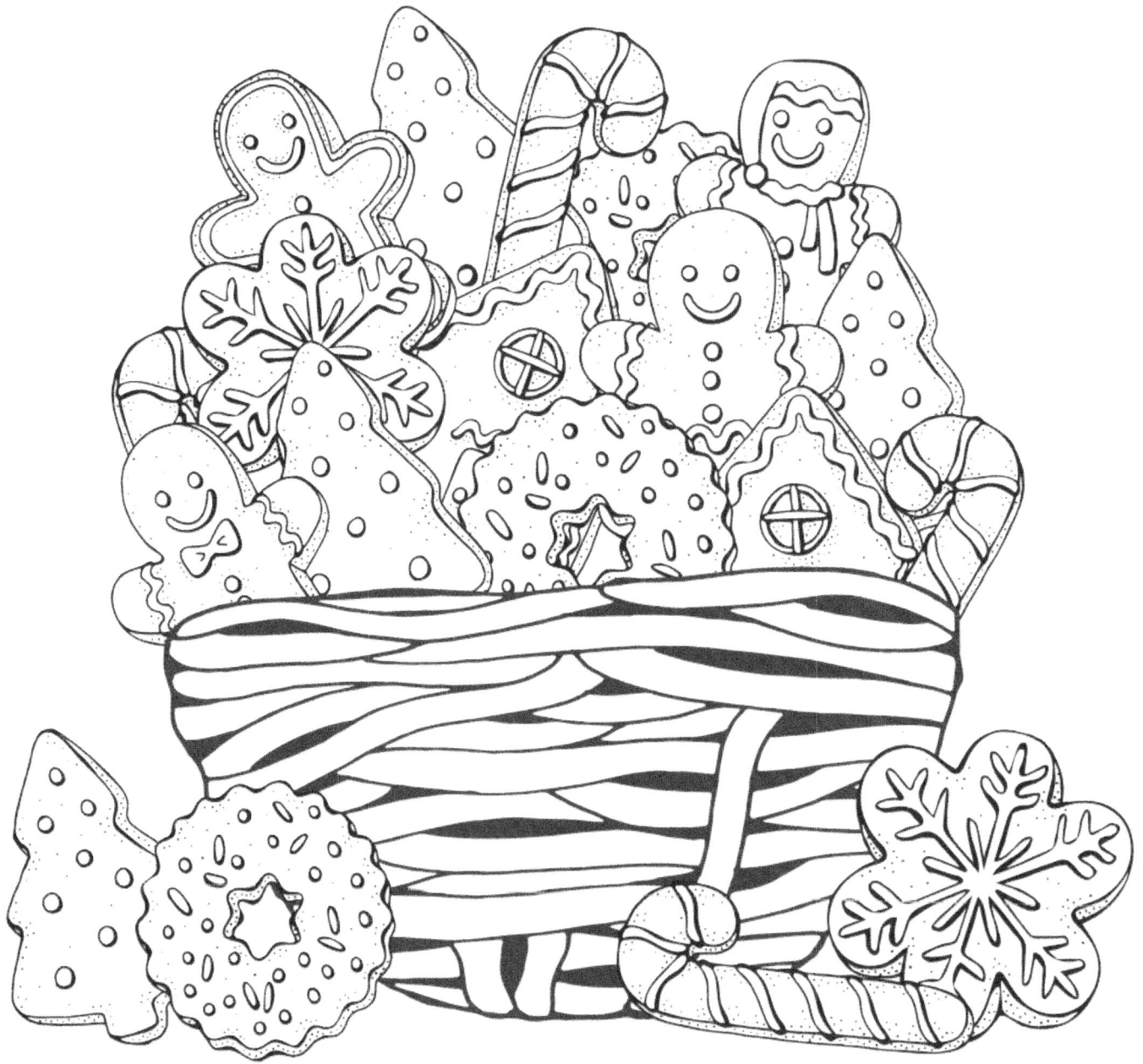

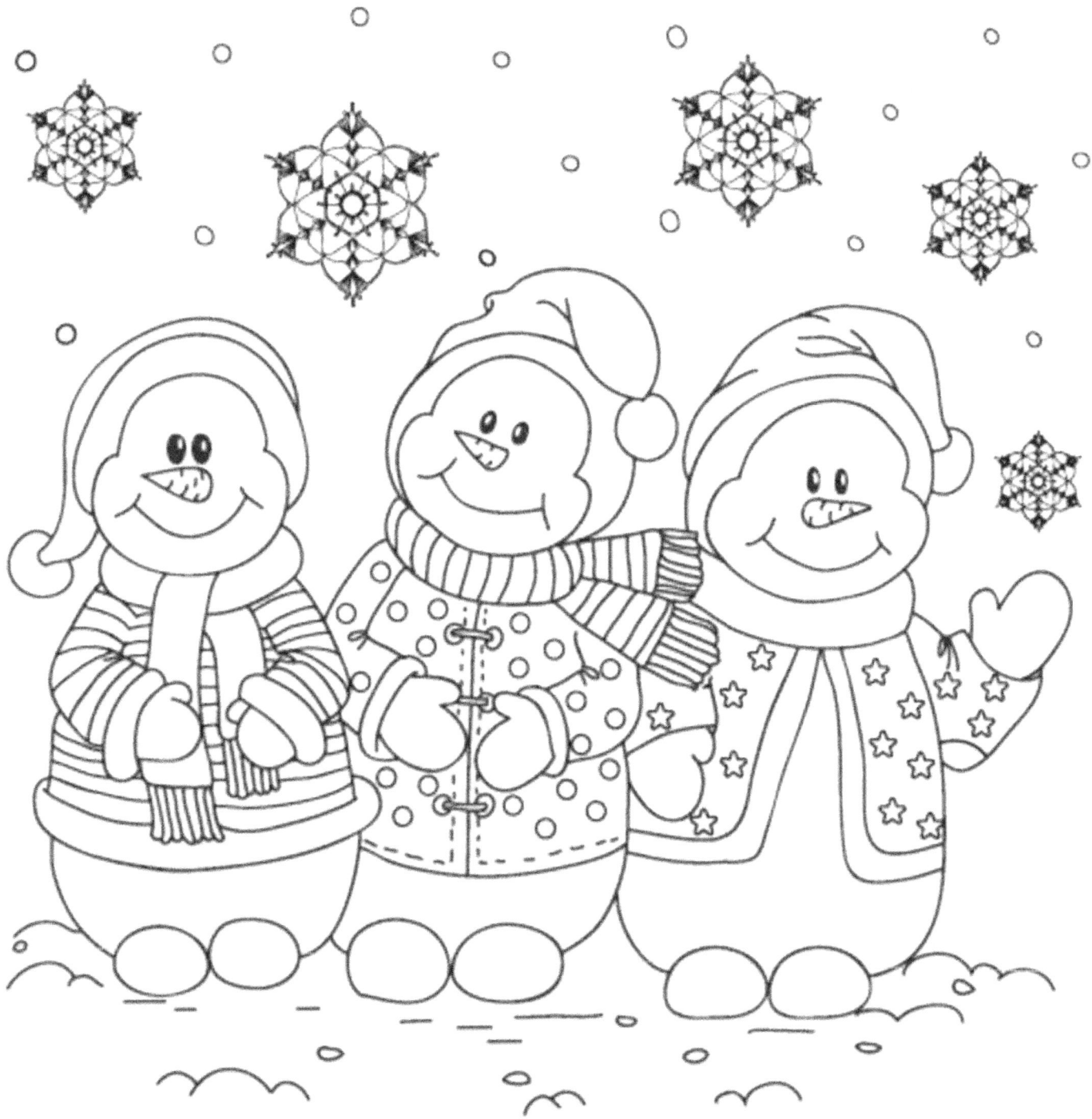

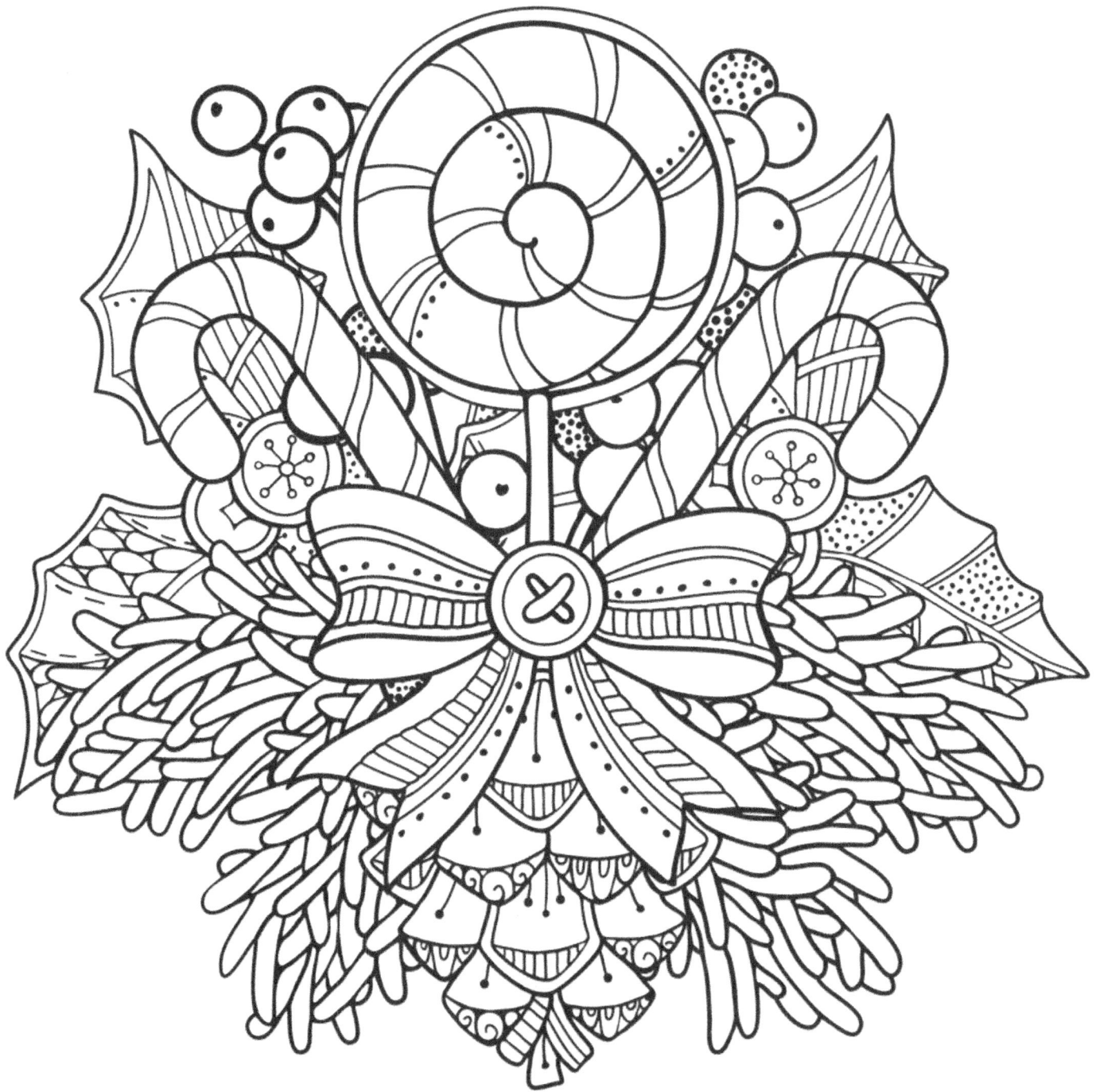

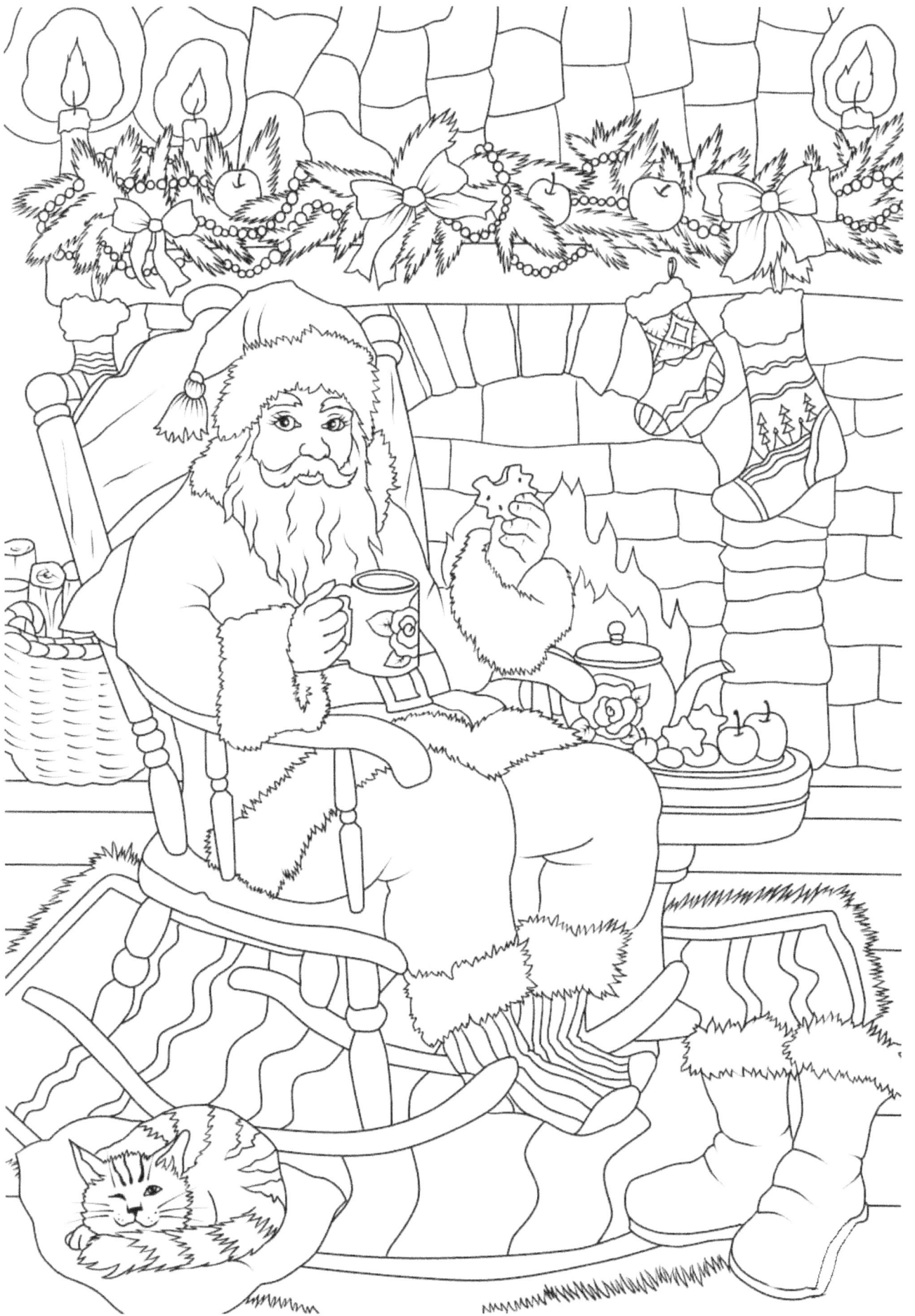

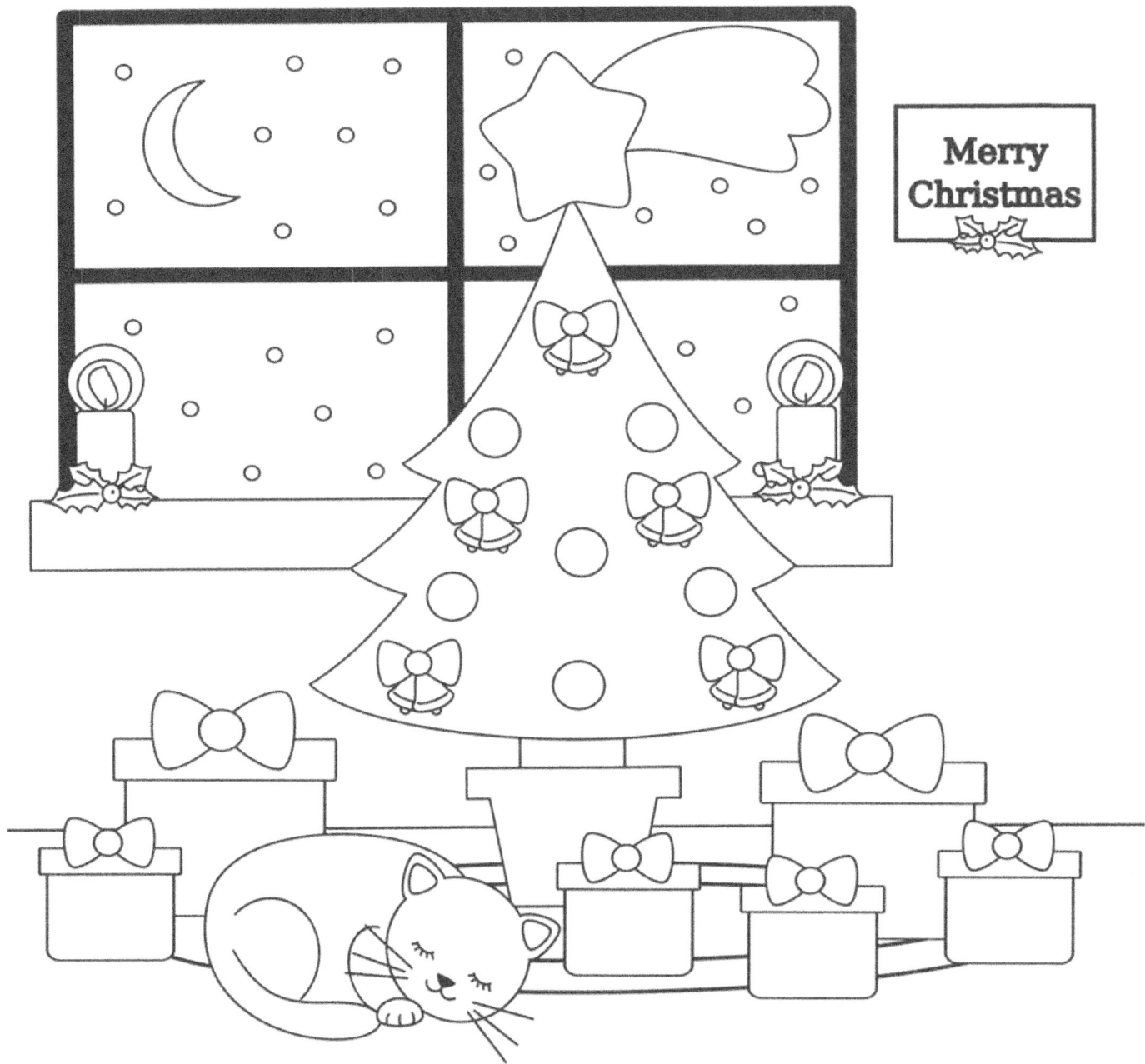

Merry Christmas

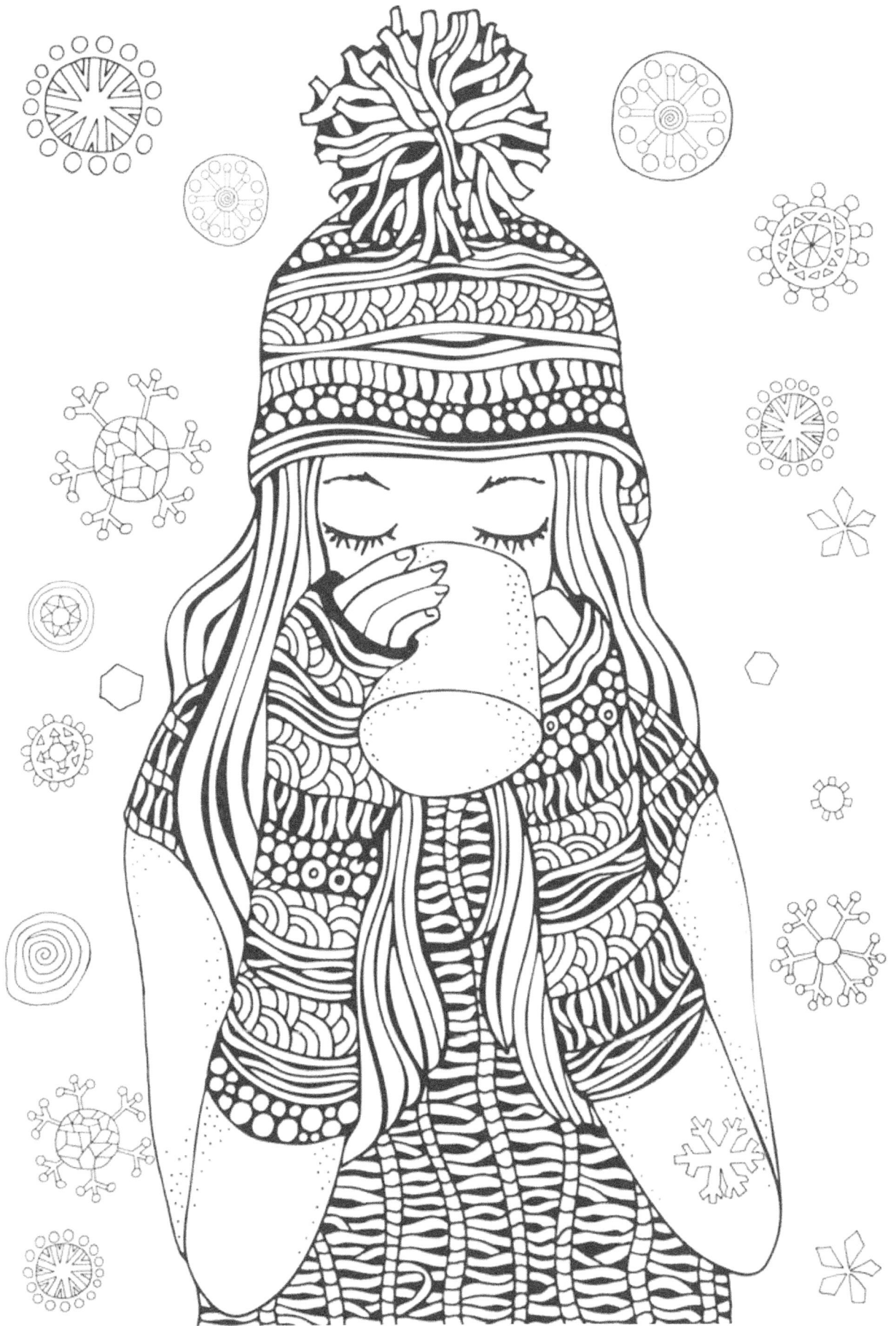

Your Own Art

Your Own Art

Your Own Art

Your Own Art

Your Own Art

Your Own Art

Write Your Experience

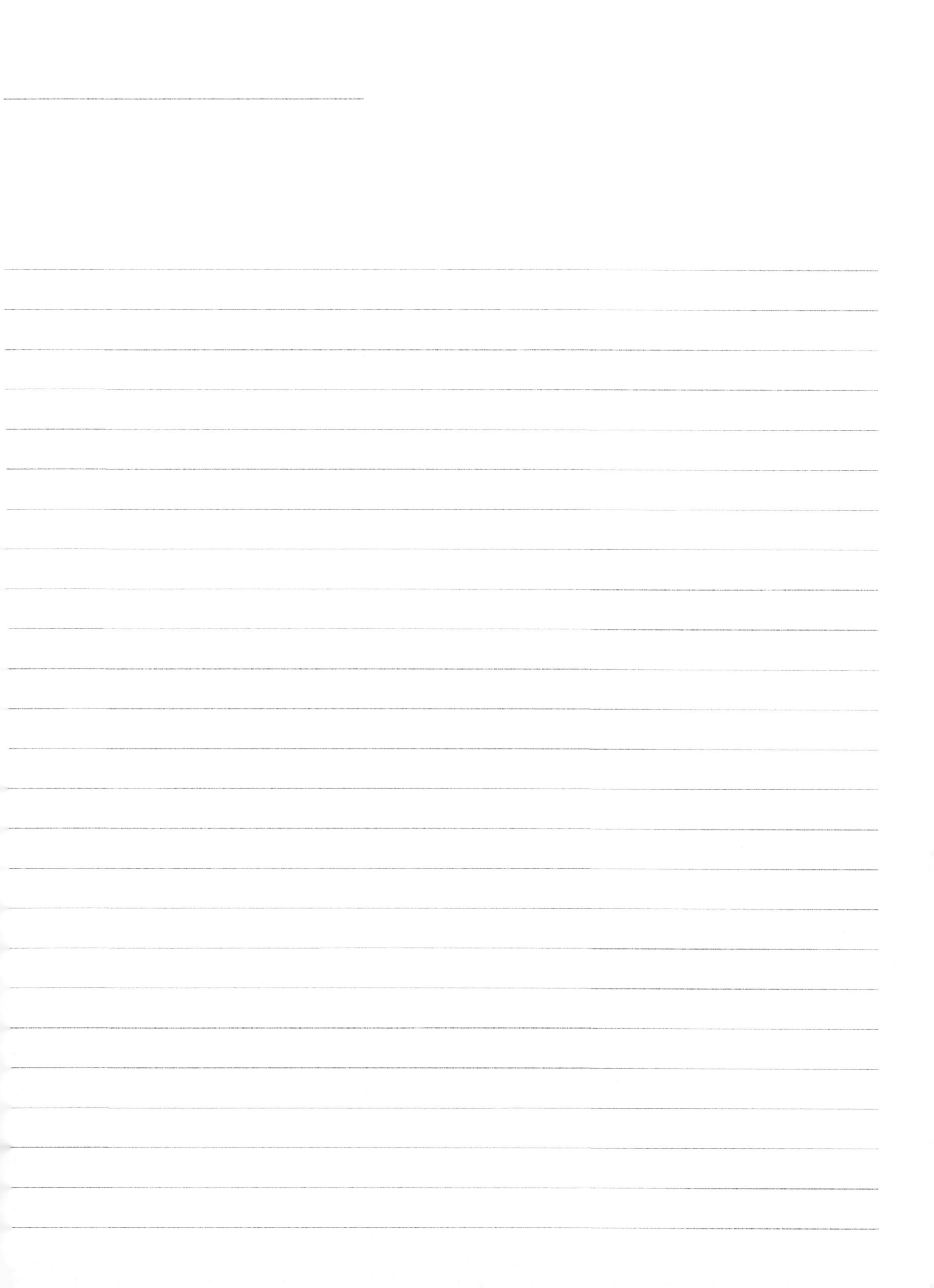

Made in the USA
Las Vegas, NV
24 October 2023